Certified Kubernetes Application Developer (CKAD) Study Guide
In-Depth Guidance and Practice

Benjamin Muschko

Beijing · Boston · Farnham · Sebastopol · Tokyo

Certified Kubernetes Application Developer (CKAD) Study Guide

by Benjamin Muschko

Published by O'Reilly Media, Inc., 1005 Gravenstein Highway North, Sebastopol, CA 95472.

O'Reilly books may be purchased for educational, business, or sales promotional use. Online editions are also available for most titles (*http://oreilly.com*). For more information, contact our corporate/institutional sales department: 800-998-9938 or *corporate@oreilly.com*.

Acquisitions Editor: John Devins
Development Editor: Michele Cronin
Production Editor: Beth Kelly
Copyeditor: Holly Bauer Forsyth
Proofreader: Justin Billing

Indexer: Judy McConville
Interior Designer: David Futato
Cover Designer: Karen Montgomery
Illustrator: Kate Dullea

February 2021:   First Edition

Revision History for the First Edition
2021-02-02:   First Release

See *http://oreilly.com/catalog/errata.csp?isbn=9781492083733* for release details.

978-1-492-08373-3

[LSI]

Table of Contents

Preface

Microservices architecture is one of the hottest areas of application development today, particularly for cloud-based, enterprise-scale applications. The benefits of building applications using small, single-purpose services are well documented. But managing what can sometimes be enormous numbers of containerized services is no easy task and requires the addition of an "orchestrator" to keep it all together. Kubernetes is among the most popular and broadly used tools for this job, so it's no surprise that the ability to use, troubleshoot, and monitor Kubernetes as an application developer is in high demand. To help job seekers and employers have a standard means to demonstrate and evaluate proficiency in developing with a Kubernetes environment, the Cloud Native Computing Foundation (CNCF) developed the Certified Kubernetes Application Developer (CKAD) (*https://oreil.ly/sq-Po*) program. To achieve this certification, you need to pass an exam.

The CKAD is not to be confused with the Certified Kubernetes Administrator (CKA) (*https://oreil.ly/-uTol*). While there is an overlap of topics, the CKA focuses mostly on Kubernetes cluster adminstration tasks rather than developing applications operated in a cluster.

In this study guide, I will explore the topics covered in the CKAD exam to fully prepare you to pass the certification exam. We'll look at determining when and how you should apply the core concepts of Kubernetes to manage an application. We'll also examine the kubectl command-line tool, a mainstay of the Kubernetes engineer. I will also offer tips to help you better prepare for the exam and share my personal experience with getting ready for all aspects of it.

The CKAD is different from the typical multiple-choice format of other certifications. It's completely performance based and requires you to demonstrate deep knowledge of the tasks at hand under immense time pressure. Are you ready to pass the test on the first go?

Who This Book Is For

The primary target group for this book is developers who want to prepare for the CKAD exam. The content covers all aspects of the exam curriculum, though basic knowledge of the Kubernetes architecture and its concepts is expected. If you are completely new to Kubernetes, I recommend reading *Kubernetes Up & Running* (*https://oreil.ly/mwKc-*) by Brendan Burns, Joe Beda, and Kelsey Hightower (O'Reilly) or *Kubernetes in Action* by Marko Lukša (Manning Publications) first.

What You Will Learn

The content of the book condenses the most important aspects relevant to the CKAD exam. Given the plethora of configuration options available in Kubernetes, it's almost impossible to cover all use cases and scenarios without duplicating the official documentation. Test takers are encouraged to reference the Kubernetes documentation (*https://kubernetes.io/docs/home*) as the go-to compendium for broader exposure.

The outline of the book follows the CKAD curriculum to a tee. While there might be a more natural, didactical structure for learning Kubernetes in general, the curriculum outline will help test takers with preparing for the exam by focusing on specific topics. As a result, you will find yourself cross-referencing other chapters of the book depending on your existing knowledge level.

Be aware that this book only covers the concepts relevant to the CKAD exam. Certain primitives that you may expect to be covered by the certification curriculum—for example, the API primitive Ingress—are not discussed. Refer to the Kubernetes documentation or other books if you want to dive deeper.

Practical experience with Kubernetes is key to passing the exam. Each chapter contains a section named "Sample Exercises" with practice questions. Solutions to those questions can be found in the Appendix.

Conventions Used in This Book

The following typographical conventions are used in this book:

Italic
> Indicates new terms, URLs, email addresses, filenames, and file extensions.

`Constant width`
> Used for program listings, as well as within paragraphs to refer to program elements such as variable or function names, databases, data types, environment variables, statements, and keywords.

Constant width bold

    Shows commands or other text that should be typed literally by the user.

Constant width italic

    Shows text that should be replaced with user-supplied values or by values determined by context.

 This element signifies a tip or suggestion.

 This element signifies a general note.

 This element indicates a warning or caution.

Using Code Examples

The source code for all examples and exercises in this book is available on GitHub (*https://github.com/bmuschko/ckad-study-guide*). The repository is distributed under the Apache License 2.0. The code is free to use in commercial and open source projects. If you encounter an issue in the source code or if you have a question, open an issue in the GitHub issue tracker (*https://oreil.ly/WKl2y*). I'll be happy to have a conversation and fix any issues that might arise.

This book is here to help you get your job done. In general, if example code is offered with this book, you may use it in your programs and documentation. You do not need to contact us for permission unless you're reproducing a significant portion of the code. For example, writing a program that uses several chunks of code from this book does not require permission. Selling or distributing examples from O'Reilly books does require permission. Answering a question by citing this book and quoting example code does not require permission. Incorporating a significant amount of example code from this book into your product's documentation does require permission.

We appreciate, but generally do not require, attribution. An attribution usually includes the title, author, publisher, and ISBN. For example: "*Certified Kubernetes Application Developer (CKAD) Study Guide* by Benjamin Muschko (O'Reilly). Copyright 2021 Automated Ascent, LLC, 978-1-492-08373-3."

If you feel your use of code examples falls outside fair use or the permission given above, feel free to contact us at *permissions@oreilly.com*.

O'Reilly Online Learning

 For more than 40 years, *O'Reilly Media* has provided technology and business training, knowledge, and insight to help companies succeed.

Our unique network of experts and innovators share their knowledge and expertise through books, articles, and our online learning platform. O'Reilly's online learning platform gives you on-demand access to live training courses, in-depth learning paths, interactive coding environments, and a vast collection of text and video from O'Reilly and 200+ other publishers. For more information, visit *http://oreilly.com*.

How to Contact Us

Please address comments and questions concerning this book to the publisher:

O'Reilly Media, Inc.
1005 Gravenstein Highway North
Sebastopol, CA 95472
800-998-9938 (in the United States or Canada)
707-829-0515 (international or local)
707-829-0104 (fax)

We have a web page for this book, where we list errata, examples, and any additional information. You can access this page at *https://oreil.ly/ckad*.

Email *bookquestions@oreilly.com* to comment or ask technical questions about this book.

For news and information about our books and courses, visit *http://oreilly.com*.

Find us on Facebook: *http://facebook.com/oreilly*

Follow us on Twitter: *http://twitter.com/oreillymedia*

Watch us on YouTube: *http://youtube.com/oreillymedia*

Follow the author on Twitter: *https://twitter.com/bmuschko*

Follow the author on GitHub: *https://github.com/bmuschko*

Follow the author's blog: *https://bmuschko.com*

Acknowledgments

Every book project is a long journey and would not be possible without the help of the editorial staff and technical reviewers. Special thanks go to Jonathon Johnson, Mohammed Hewedy, Sebastien Goasguen, Michael Hausenblaus, and Peter Miron for their detailed technical guidance and feedback. I would also like to thank the editors at O'Reilly Media, John Devins and Michele Cronin, for their continued support and encouragement.

## CHAPTER 1

Exam Details and Resources

In this introductory chapter, I want to address the most burning questions frequently asked by candidates planning to prepare and successfully pass the Certified Kubernetes Application Developer (CKAD) (*https://oreil.ly/sq-Po*) exam. We won't discuss the actual Kubernetes concepts or how to apply them yet, but rather talk about the certification and the necessary skills at a high level.

Exam Objectives

More and more application developers find themselves in projects transitioning from a monolithic architectural model to bite-sized, cohesive, and containerized microservices. There are pros and cons to both approaches, but we can't deny that Kubernetes has become the de facto runtime platform for deploying and operating applications without needing to worry about the underlying physical infrastructure.

Nowadays, it's no longer the exclusive responsibility of an administrator or release manager to deploy and monitor their applications in target runtime environments. Application developers need to see their applications through from development to operation. Some organizations like Netflix live and breathe this culture, so you, the application developer, are fully responsible for making design decisions as well as fixing issues in production. It's more important than ever to understand the capabilities of Kubernetes, how to apply the relevant concepts properly, and how to interact with the platform.

The CKAD exam has been designed specifically for application developers who need to design, build, configure, and manage cloud native applications on Kubernetes.

Kubernetes version used during the exam

At the time of writing, the exam is based on Kubernetes 1.19. All content in this book will follow the features, APIs, and command-line support for that specific version. It's certainly possible that future versions will break backward compatibility. While preparing for the certification, review the Kubernetes release notes (*https://oreil.ly/dbSMp*) and practice with the Kubernetes version used during the exam to avoid unpleasant surprises.

Curriculum

At a high level, the curriculum covers the following topics. Each topic carries a different weight when it comes to the overall score:

- 13% – Core Concepts
- 18% – Configuration
- 10% – Multi-Container Pods
- 18% – Observability
- 20% – Pod Design
- 13% – Services & Networking
- 8% – State Persistence

The outline of the book follows the CKAD curriculum to a tee. While there might be a more natural, didactical organization structure to learn Kubernetes in general, the curriculum outline will help test takers with preparing for the exam by focusing on specific topics. As a result, you will find yourself cross-referencing other chapters of the book depending on your existing knowledge level.

Let's break down each domain in detail and identify what they actually entail.

Core Concepts

The Kubernetes environment is defined by a collection of objects, also called primitives. Each Kubernetes object represents a specific functionality of the system. Why are they called "objects," you might ask? In the very early days of Kubernetes, the source code was implemented in Java, which has the concept of classes to represent specific types in the system. The code has since been written in Go, but the terminology remained. This portion of the exam covers the general structure of a Kubernetes object and its representation in YAML. You'll need to be familiar with the different ways to create, delete, and modify a Kubernetes object from the command line. The most important object in the Kubernetes object model is a Pod. A Pod is what you use to deploy an application and run it in a container. This section focuses on the basics of Pod management: creating, configuring, and inspecting Pods.

Configuration

This section of the exam drills into the advanced configuration options for Pods, primarily with the help of other Kubernetes objects. ConfigMaps and Secrets help with centralizing configuration data needed by a Pod at runtime. You will have to understand how to create and use both concepts. Furthermore, this section covers the ins and outs of defining privileges and access control for containers using a security context. A ResourceQuota limits the amount of resources like CPU and memory granted to a namespace. As part of the exam, you will need to know how to define such a resource limit as well as minimum and maximum resource boundaries for a container. Finally, this section covers Service Accounts, the Kubernetes objects that allow defining the identities for processes running in a Pod.

Multi-Container Pods

Oftentimes, Pods only contain a single container. There are viable use cases that require running multiple containers in a Pod. For the exam, you will need to understand init containers and the various established patterns for multi-container Pods. The curriculum explicitly spells out three patterns you need to be familiar with: the sidecar pattern, the adapter pattern, and the ambassador pattern.

Observability

Containers don't always walk the happy path. Like in real life, things can go wrong, and that's OK; however, we'll need to be able to deal with it appropriately. Kubernetes provides readiness, liveness, and startup probes that can identify the health state of the application running in the container and potentially act accordingly to correct a failure situation. Sometimes, there's no way around digging deep. You will have to understand how to debug containers that failed with proven mitigation strategies. While this section also covers monitoring, it's not very high on the list of exam topics, as it requires the use of commercial products. Its relevance to the exam is likely insignificant.

Pod Design

Labels are an integral concept in Kubernetes. They are key-value pairs used for querying, sorting, and filtering Kubernetes objects. While annotations look similar to labels on the surface, they serve a different purpose. For the exam, you will need to understand labels and annotations and how to apply the concepts to solve different use cases. This section also covers Deployments, so make sure you fully understand the replication and scalability features of a Deployment. Moreover, practice the use of Jobs for running batch-processing operations and CronJobs for operations that should run at specific times.

Services & Networking

A services is an abstraction layer on top of a set of Pods that provides a single interface for defining the network communication. You will need to understand how to create such a Service, its port-mapping mechanism, as well as the different types of Services. Network policies describe the access rules for incoming and outgoing traffic for Pods. In the context of defining network policies, get a good handle on label selectors, port rules, and the typical use cases that may benefit from applying the network policies to strengthen security.

State Persistence

Applications in a container perform file I/O only to the container's file system. If the read/write location is not associated to an external mount, then the files are lost at the end of the container's life. This section covers the different types of volumes for reading and writing data. Learn how to create and configure them. Persistent Volumes ensure permanent data persistence even beyond a cluster node restart. You will need to be familiar with the mechanics and how to mount a Persistent Volume to a path in a container.

The main purpose of the exam is to test your practical knowledge of Kubernetes primitives. It is to be expected that the exam combines multiple concepts in a single problem. Refer to Figure 1-1 as a rough guide to the applicable Kubernetes resources and their relationships.

You might have noticed that the exam does not cover all the Kubernetes resources you would have expected to find in the diagram. Certain Kubernetes primitives like ReplicaSet, StatefulSet, or Ingress did not find their way into the curriculum, which means do you not necessarily have to study them. Nevertheless, it's a good idea to get a good lay of the land and understand the most prominent concepts at a high level.

While this book covers all Kubernetes resources shown in the diagram, it's almost impossible to explain all imaginable scenarios and configuration options. Use the information explained in the following chapters as a starting point to dive deeper. Don't be afraid to explore uncharted territory!

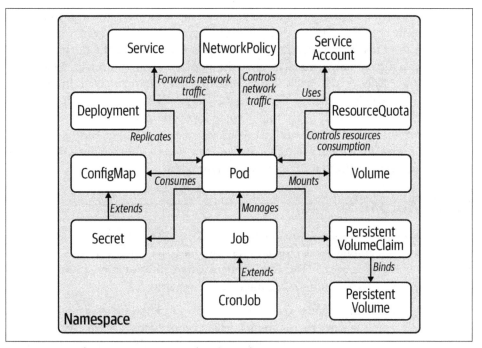

Figure 1-1. Kubernetes primitives relevant to the exam

Exam Environment and Tips

The exam is conducted and proctored online. As a result, you can register and take the exam from the comfort of your home. It's recommended that you clear your desk and ensure a silent environment by preventing any interruptions by other people or distracting noises. An exam representative will watch over you via video and audio. Cheating attempts will result in your exam being terminated prematurely.

The exam consists of practical problems you have to solve within a two-hour time frame. You will work on a preconfigured set of Kubernetes clusters. The focus of the exercises is to simulate typical situations you would encounter as an application developer using Kubernetes.

Once you enter the exam environment, you are presented with a web-based command-line environment. Most of your interaction happens inside of that terminal. I personally felt that the terminal was a bit laggy—whatever I typed didn't show up on screen until a split second later. Be aware that the terminal does not provide any sophisticated auto-completion functionality for kubectl commands.

You are permitted to access and browse the Kubernetes documentation (*https://kuber netes.io/docs*) in single browser tab. In preparation for the exam, read through the bulk of the information at least once. While you can reference anything in the documentation, know where and how to find relevant iinformation to avoid spending too much time browsing. Do not open links to external web pages, even if they're referenced in the Kubernetes documentation. I made heavy use of the documentation page's search functionality, which helped me find the right information based on search terms quickly. Additionally, I would like to point you to two gems in the documentation: the kubectl cheat sheet (*https://oreil.ly/3wgkY*) and the API reference (*https://oreil.ly/d-Pdt*). Both pages might come in handy as quick reference guides. You can't print these out beforehand, but you can have one tab open during the exam. For more information about the exam environment, see the Frequently Asked Questions (*https://oreil.ly/br0Gv*) for the certification program.

Candidate Skills

The certification assumes that you already have a basic understanding of Kubernetes. You should be familiar with Kubernetes internals, its core concepts, and the command-line tool kubectl. The CNCF offers a free "Introduction to Kubernetes" course (*https://oreil.ly/GJ1mp*) for beginners to Kubernetes.

Your background is likely more on the end of an application developer, although it doesn't really matter which programming language you're most accustomed to. Here's a brief overview of the background knowledge you should bring to the table to increase your likelihood of passing the exam:

Kubernetes architecture and concepts
> The CKAD exam won't ask you to install a Kubernetes cluster from scratch. Read up on the basics of Kubernetes and its architectural components. Don't expect to encounter any multiple-choice questions during the exam.

The kubectl CLI tool
> The kubectl command-line tool is the central tool you will use during the exam to interact with the Kubernetes cluster. Even if you only have a little time to prepare for the exam, it's essential to practice how to operate kubectl, as well as its commands and their relevant options. You will have no access to the web dashboard UI (*https://oreil.ly/2tZBk*) during the exam.

Working knowledge of Docker
> Kubernetes uses Docker by default for managing images. You are not expected to run Docker commands, though it's useful to understand its basic concepts and know how to operate it from the command line. At a minimum, understand Dockerfiles, images, containers, and their corresponding CLI commands.

Other relevant tools
> Kubernetes objects are represented by YAML or JSON. The content of this book will only use examples in YAML, as it is more commonly used than JSON in the

Kubernetes world. You will have to edit YAML during the exam to create a new object declaratively or when modifying the configuration of a live object. Ensure that you have a good handle on basic YAML syntax, data types, and indentation conforming to the specification. How do you edit the YAML definitions, you may ask? From the terminal, of course. The exam terminal environment comes with the tools vi and vim preinstalled. Practice the keyboard shortcuts for common operations, (especially how to exit the editor). The last tool I want to mention is GNU Bash. It's imperative that you understand the basic syntax and operators of the scripting language. It's absolutely possible that you may have read, modify, or even extend a multiline Bash command running in a container.

Time Management

I mentioned earlier that you'll have two hours to solve the problems presented to you. While two hours sounds like a long time, in reality, it isn't. To be precise, you have an average of 6.4 minutes per problem. The exam is very time constrained on purpose. It's designed to put you under pressure to ensure that your knowledge of Kubernetes has been deeply ingrained into muscle memory.

I can provide you with a couple of time-management tips that helped me get the most out of my alloted time. The exam presents you with a mix of questions with varying degrees of complexity. It's a good idea to start with question one. If you can't solve the issue right away or only partially, move on to the next question. Sooner or later you will encounter a problem you can solve quickly and confidently. Solving easy problems first will help you score the points you need to pass.

There's no value in getting stuck on a hard question and wasting too much time. When taking the exam myself, I left one question completely unsolved and one question only partially solved before I ran out of time. Nevertheless, I passed, which speaks to staying laser-focused on scoring points.

Taking notes

The exam environment provides a little notepad you can use to track unsolved problems. Simply mark down the questions you are planning to revisit later.

Command Line Tips and Tricks

Let me give you some additional tips and tricks for operating the command line. Not only did they help me with time management, but also with avoiding missteps during the exam.

ıg a Context and Namespace

question in the exam will ask you to operate on the exam-provided Kubernetes
and namespace. The introductory text of the question clearly states the command you need to run. Don't forget to execute the command, especially if you are
rapidly jumping back and forth between different questions.

You may not be working with namespaces in Kubernetes on a day-to-day basis, especially in smaller organizations, which may simply manage Kubernetes objects in the
default namespace. The exam makes heavy use of custom namespaces. You can
decide to spell out the namespace for every single command while working through
the exam; however, this mode of operation comes at the risk of forgetting to set the
namespace.

To avoid issues, run the following command once before working through the steps
of a question. The command sets the context and the namespace at the same time:

```
$ kubectl config set-context <context-of-question> \
  --namespace=<namespace-of-question>
```

Using an Alias for kubectl

The kubectl command-line tool is your primary interface to the Kubernetes cluster.
For every command you need to execute, you will have to type kubectl in the terminal. No big deal, you might say. Do yourself a favor and define a shell alias as a shortcut to reference the kubectl command. I personally prefer to use the single letter
command, k. You will only need to set the alias once at the beginning of the exam to
shave off a couple of seconds for every command you run going forward:

```
$ alias k=kubectl
$ k version
```

I'm going to continue to use the full kubectl command throughout the other chapters to avoid confusing those who didn't reference this particular section.

Internalize Resource Short Names

Some Kubernetes resources have excruciatingly long names. Just imagine having to
type persistentvolumeclaims every time you need to reference the Kubernetes
resource Persistent Volume Claim. Thankfully, kubectl provides short names for
some of the resources. The following command lists all of them in the terminal:

```
$ kubectl api-resources
NAME                     SHORTNAMES  APIGROUP  NAMESPACED  KIND
...
persistentvolumeclaims   pvc                   true        PersistentVolumeClaim
...
```

You can see in the output that `persistentvolumeclaims` offers the short name `pvc`. Consequently, a command that interacts with a Persistent Volume Claim could look as simple as this:

```
$ kubectl describe pvc my-claim
```

Deleting Kubernetes Objects

It's inevitable that you will make mistakes during the exam. For example, you might create Kubernetes objects with incorrect configuration, or you may simply want to start a question over from scratch. By default, Kubernetes tries to delete objects gracefully, which can can take up to 30 seconds. Given that we're dealing with a test environment, there's no point in waiting. Use the command line option `--grace-period=0` and `--force` to send a `SIGKILL` signal. The signal will delete a Kubernetes object immediately:

```
$ kubectl delete pod nginx --grace-period=0 --force
```

Finding Object Information

Some questions in the exam present you with an existing setup of Kubernetes objects. Don't be surprised to find that the context you're working in already contains a couple of Pods with non-trivial configuration. As part of the question, you may be asked to identify specific Kubernetes objects and continue to work on those.

You can always inspect Kubernetes objects one by one, but again, this would be a major time sink. It is helpful to remember that you can combine a `kubectl` command with other Unix commands using a pipe call. For example, you could run a `describe pods` command and then filter the output with the `grep` command to find assigned labels. The `-C` command-line option helps with rendering the lines before and after the search term:

```
$ kubectl describe pods | grep -C 10 "author=John Doe"
$ kubectl get pods -o yaml | grep -C 5 labels:
```

Discovering Command Options

Even though you have access to the Kubernetes documentation, you might not be able to find the exact information you're looking for right away. The `kubectl` command has help functionality built in. The option `--help` works for every command available and renders details on subcommands, command-line options, and usage examples. The following command demonstrates its use for the `create` command:

```
$ kubectl create --help
Create a resource from a file or from stdin.

JSON and YAML formats are accepted.
```

```
Examples:
  ...

Available Commands:
  ...

Options:
  ...
```

Furthermore, you can explore the fields of every Kubernetes resource from the command line with the explain command. As a parameter, you have to provide the JSONPath for the field of interest. For example, say you wanted to list all fields of a Pod's spec; you would use the following command:

```
$ kubectl explain pods.spec
KIND:     Pod
VERSION:  v1

RESOURCE: spec <Object>

DESCRIPTION:
  ...

FIELDS:
  ...
```

Practicing and Practice Exams

In preparation for the exam, it's essential to practice using kubectl. You'll need to have access to a Kubernetes cluster and kubectl preinstalled. Consider the following options:

- Find out if your employer already has a Kubernetes cluster set up and will allow you to use it to practice.

- Installing Kubernetes on your developer machine is an easy and fast way to get set up. The Kubernetes documentation provides various installation options (*https://oreil.ly/jA165*), depending on your operating system. At some point during my Kubernetes learning journey, I installed Kubernetes on four Raspberry Pis, which turned out to be a fun and exciting hobby project. You can find information on how to get started on the Kubernetes blog (*https://oreil.ly/iCOdP*).

- If you're a subscriber to the O'Reilly Learning Platform (*https://oreil.ly/OLP*), you have unlimited access to scenarios running a Kubernetes environment in Katacoda (*https://oreil.ly/Uucxp*).

In addition, you may also want to try out one of the following free or paid practice exams:

- The Certified Kubernetes Application Developer (CKAD) Prep Course (*https:// oreil.ly/MFAjT*) is a video-based Learning Path on the O'Reilly Learning Platform, created by yours truly.
- Certified Kubernetes Application Developer (CKAD) Cert Prep: Exam Tips (*https://oreil.ly/MPofV*) is a video-based course on LinkedIn Learning that focuses exclusively on exam preparation.
- CKAD Exercises (*https://oreil.ly/G4hOP*) is a GitHub repository containing a variety of free exercises that span all topics relevant to the curriculum.
- Other online training providers offer video courses for the CKAD exam, some of which include an integrated Kubernetes practice environment. I would like to mention KodeKloud (*https://oreil.ly/hHYyi*) and Linux Academy (*https://oreil.ly/ ute7r*). You'll need to purchase a subscription to access the content for each course individually.

Summary

The CKAD exam is a completely hands-on test that requires you to solve problems in multiple Kubernetes clusters. You're expected to understand, use, and configure the Kubernetes primitives relevant to application developers. The exam curriculum subdivides those focus areas and puts different weights on topics, which determines their contributions to the overall score. Even though focus areas are grouped in a meaningful fashion, the curriculum doesn't necessarily follow a natural learning path, so it's helpful to cross-reference chapters in the book in preparation for the exam.

In this chapter, we discussed the exam environment and how to navigate it. We also went over tips and tricks that can help you save time. In preparation for the exam, explore the architectural basics of Docker and Kubernetes. The key to acing the exam is intense practice of kubectl to solve real-world scenarios. The following chapters will provide you with sample exam exercises. For full exposure, reference the resources provided in "Practicing and Practice Exams" on page 10.

## CHAPTER 2

Core Concepts

By "core concepts," the CKAD curriculum is referring to Kubernetes' basic concepts, its API, and the commands to operate an application on Kubernetes. In this chapter, we'll discuss the basic structure of Kubernetes primitives and the main entry point for interacting with them: the command line–based client, kubectl.

A Pod is the Kubernetes primitive for running an application in a container. We'll touch on the predominant aspects of a Pod and also briefly discuss Docker, the containerization technology employed by Kubernetes.

At the end of the chapter, you'll understand how to create Kubernetes objects imperatively and declaratively and know how to create a Pod and define its most basic configuration.

At a high level, this chapter covers the following concepts:

- Container concepts
- Pod
- Namespace

Kubernetes Primitives

Kubernetes primitives are the basic building blocks anchored in the Kubernetes architecture for creating and operating an application on the platform. Even as a beginner to Kubernetes, you might have heard of the terms Pod, Deployment, and Service, all of which are Kubernetes primitives. There are many more that serve a dedicated purpose in the Kubernetes architecture.

To draw an analogy, think back to the concepts of object-oriented programming. In object-oriented programming languages, a class defines the blueprint of a real-world functionality: its properties and behavior. A Kubernetes primitive is the equivalent of a class. The instance of a class in object-oriented programming is an object, managing its own state and having the ability to communicate with other parts of the system. Whenever you create a Kubernetes object, you produce such an instance.

For example, a Pod in Kubernetes is the class of which there can be many instances with their own identity. Every Kubernetes object has a system-generated unique identifier (also known as UID) to clearly distinguish between the entities of a system. Later, we'll have look at the properties of a Kubernetes object. Figure 2-1 illustrates the relationship between a Kubernetes primitive and an object.

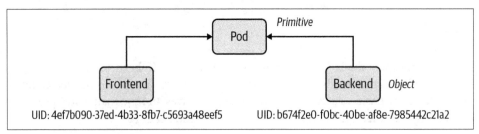

Figure 2-1. Kubernetes object identity

Each and every Kubernetes primitive follows a general structure, which you can observe if you have a deeper look at a manifest of an object, as shown in Figure 2-2. The primary markup language used for a Kubernetes manifest is YAML.

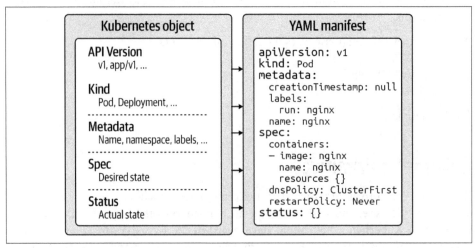

Figure 2-2. Kubernetes object structure

Let's discuss each section and its relevance within the Kubernetes system:

API version

The Kubernetes API version defines the structure of a primitive and uses it to validate the correctness of the data. The API version serves a similar purpose as XML schemas to a XML document or JSON schemas to a JSON document. The version usually undergoes a maturity process—e.g., from alpha to beta to final. Sometimes you see different prefixes separated by a slash (e.g., apps). You can list the API versions compatible with your cluster version by running the command kubectl api-versions.

Kind

The kind defines the type of primitive—e.g., a Pod or a Service. It ultimately answers the question, "What type of object are we dealing with here?"

Metadata

Metadata describes higher-level information about the object—e.g., its name, what namespace it lives in, or whether it defines labels and annotations. This section also defines the UID.

Spec

The specification ("spec" for short) declares the desired state—e.g., how should this object look after it has been created? Which image should run in the container, or which environment variables should be set for?

Status

The status describes the actual state of an object. The Kubernetes controllers and their reconcilliation loops constantly try to transition a Kubernetes object from the desired state into the actual state. The object has not yet been materialized if the YAML status shows the value {}.

With this basic structure in mind, let's have a look at how to create a Kubernetes object with the help of kubectl.

Using kubectl to Interact with the Kubernetes Cluster

kubectl is the primary tool to interact with the Kubernetes clusters from the command line. The CKAD exam is exclusively focused on the use of kubectl. Therefore, it's paramount to understand its ins and outs and practice its use heavily.

In this section, I want to provide you with a brief overview of its typical usage pattern. Let's start by looking at the syntax for running commands first. A kubectl execution consists of a command, a resource type, a resource name, and optional command line flags:

```
$ kubectl [command] [TYPE] [NAME] [flags]
```

The command specifies the operation you're planning to run. Typical commands are verbs like `create`, `get`, `describe`, or `delete`. Next, you'll need to provide the resource type you're working on, either as a full resource type or its short form. For example, you could work on a `service` here, or use the short form, `svc`. The name of the resource identifies the user-facing object identifier, effectively the value of `meta data.name` in the YAML representation. Be aware that the object name is not the same as the UID. The UID is an autogenerated, Kubernetes-internal object reference that you usually don't have to interact with. The name of an object has to be unique across all objects of the same resource type within a namespace. Finally, you can provide zero to many command line flags to describe additional configuration behavior. A typical example of a command-line flag is the `--port` flag, which exposes a Pod's container port.

Figure 2-3 shows a full `kubectl` command in action.

Figure 2-3. Kubectl usage pattern

Over the course of this book, we'll explore the `kubectl` commands that will make you the most productive during the CKAD exam. There are many more, however, and they usually go beyond the ones you'd use on a day-to-day basis as an application developer. Next up, we'll have a deeper look at the `create` command, the imperative way to create a Kubernetes object. We'll also compare the imperative object creation approach with the declarative approach.

Object Management

You can create objects in a Kubernetes cluster in two ways: imperatively or declaratively. The following sections will describe each approach, including their benefits, drawbacks, and use cases.

Imperative Approach

The imperative method for object creation does not require a manifest definition. You would use the `kubectl run` or `kubectl create` command to create an object on the fly. Any configuration needed at runtime is provided by command-line options. The benefit of this approach is the fast turnaround time without the need to wrestle with YAML structures:

```
$ kubectl run frontend --image=nginx --restart=Never --port=80
pod/frontend created
```

Declarative Approach

The declarative approach creates objects from a manifest file (in most cases, a YAML file) using the kubectl create or kubectl apply command. The benefit of using the declarative method is reproducibility and improved maintenance, as the file is checked into version control in most cases. The declarative approach is the recommended way to create objects in production environments:

```
$ vim pod.yaml
$ kubectl create -f pod.yaml
pod/frontend created
```

Hybrid Approach

Sometimes, you may want to go with a hybrid approach. You can start by using the imperative method to produce a manifest file without actually creating an object. You do so by executing the kubectl run command with the command-line options -o yaml and --dry-run=client:

```
$ kubectl run frontend --image=nginx --restart=Never --port=80 \
  -o yaml --dry-run=client > pod.yaml
$ vim pod.yaml
$ kubectl create -f pod.yaml
pod/frontend created
$ kubectl describe pod frontend
Name:        frontend
Namespace:   default
Priority:    0
...
```

Which Approach to Use?

In earlier Kubernetes versions, you were still able to create objects other than Pods with the kubectl run command. For example, with the right combination of command line options you could create Deployments and CronJobs, however, kubectl run rendered a deprecation message to remind you that support for it will go away in a future version.

Kubernetes 1.18 only allows creating Pods with the run command now. You will have to use the kubectl create command for imperatively creating any other primitive. You will find a lot of CKAD preparation material on the web that still uses the kubectl run pattern. This will not work in the exam environment anymore as the Kubernetes version has already been upgraded beyond the point of version 1.18.

While creating objects imperatively to optimize the turnaround time, in practice you'll most certainly want to rather use the declarative approach. A YAML manifest file represents the ultimate source of truth of a Kubernetes object. Version-controlled files can be audited, shared and store a history of changes in case you need to revert to a previous revision.

Other Notable Commands

So far we only talked about object creation with the imperative and declarative approach using the `run` and `create` command. The `kubectl` executable offers other notable commands in the realm of object management.

Deleting an object

At any given time, you can delete a Kubernetes object. During the exam, the need may arise if you made a mistake while solving a problem and want to start from scratch to ensure a clean slate. In a work environment, you'll want to delete objects that are not needed anymore. The `delete` command offers two options: deleting an object by providing the name or deleting an object by pointing to the YAML manifest that created it:

```
$ kubectl delete pod frontend
pod "frontend" deleted
$ kubectl delete -f pod.yaml
pod "frontend" deleted
```

Editing a live object

Say you already created an object and you wanted to make further changes to the live object. You have the option to modify the object in your editor of choice from the terminal using the `edit` command. After saving the object definition in the editor, Kubernetes will try to reflect those changes in the live object:

```
$ kubectl edit pod frontend
```

Replacing a live object

Sometimes, you'll just want to replace the definition of an existing object declaratively. The `replace` command overwrites the live configuration with the one from the provided YAML manifest. The YAML manifest you feed into the command must be a complete resource definition as observed with the `create` command:

```
$ kubectl replace -f pod.yaml
```

Updating a live object

Finally, I want to briefly explain the `apply` command and the main difference to the `create` command. The `create` command instantiates a new object. Trying to execute the `create` command for an existing object will produce an error. The `apply` command is meant to update an existing object in its entirety or just incrementally. That's why the provided YAML manifest may be a full definition of an object or a partial definition (e.g., just the number of replicas for a Deployment). Please note that the `apply` command behaves like the `create` command if the object doesn't exist yet, however, the YAML manifest will need to contain a full definition of the object:

```
$ kubectl apply -f pod.yaml
pod/frontend configured
```

In the next section, we'll put our knowledge in practice by creating and interacting with Pods.

Understanding Pods

The most important primitive in the Kubernetes API is the Pod. A Pod lets you run a containerized application. In practice, you'll often encounter a one to one mapping between a Pod and a container, however, there are use cases we'll discuss in a later chapter that benefit from declaring more than one container in a single Pod.

In addition to just running a container, a Pod can consume other services like a persistent storage, configuration data, and much more. Therefore, think of a Pod as a wrapper for running containers including the mediator functionality with other Kubernetes objects.

Before jumping deeper into the coverage of a Pod, let's first explore the role a OCI-compliant container runtime plays in the Kubernetes ecosystem. We'll use the Docker daemon as an example of such a container runtime.

Containerization Process

Kubernetes is a container orchestrator that uses a container runtime to instantiate containers inside of Pods. By default, this container runtime is the Docker. While it is not strictly necessary to understand Docker as a whole for the exam, you should at least be familiar with its basics. In this section, we'll talk about Docker's foundational concepts and commands. It is safe to skip this section if you're already familiar with Docker.

Container Concepts

A *container* packages an application into a single unit of software including its runtime environment and configuration. This unit of software usually includes the operating system, the application's source code or the binary, its dependencies and other system tools deemed necessary. The declared goal of a container is to decouple the runtime environment from the application to avoid the "works on my machine" problem.

The process of bundling an application into a container is commonly referred to as *containerization*. Containerization works based on instructions defined in a so-called

Dockerfile. The Dockerfile explicitly spells out what needs to happen when the software is built. The result of the operation is an *image*. The image is usually published to a *registry* for consumption by other stakeholders. Docker Hub (*https://hub.docker.com*) is the primary registry for Docker images available for public use. Other public registries like GCR and Quay are available. Figure 2-4 illustrates the concepts in the context of containerizing an application.

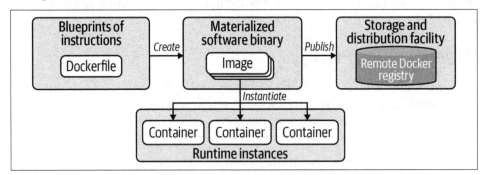

Figure 2-4. Containerization process

To summarize, the Dockerfile is a blueprint of how the software should be built, the image is the artifact produced by the process, and the container is an running instance of the image serving the application. Let's have a look at a more concrete example.

Example: Containerizing a Java-Based Application

Let's assume we'd want to containerize a web application written in Java. The application doesn't write core functionality from scratch but uses the Spring Boot framework (*https://oreil.ly/Na9Vb*) as an external library. In addition, we'll want to control the runtime behavior with the help of environment variables. For example, you may want to provide URLs and credentials to connect to other services like a database. We'll talk through the process step by step and execute the relevant Docker commands from the terminal. If you want to follow along, you can download a sample application from the project generator Spring Initalizr (*https://oreil.ly/bXSA4*).

Before we can create the image, we'll have to write a Dockerfile. The Dockerfile can reside in any directory and is essentially a plain-text file. The instructions below use the OpenJDK distribution of Java 11 as the base image. A base image contains the operating system and the necessary tooling, in this case Java. Moreover, we include the binary file, an executable Java archive (JAR), into the directory /app of the image. Finally, we define the Java command that executes the program and expose the port 8080 to make the application accessible when run in a container. Example 2-1 outlines a sample Dockerfile.

Example 2-1. Dockerfile for building a Java application

```
FROM openjdk:11-jre-slim
WORKDIR /app
COPY target/java-hello-world-0.0.1.jar java-hello-world.jar
ENTRYPOINT ["java", "-jar", "/app/java-hello-world.jar"]
EXPOSE 8080
```

With the Dockerfile in place, we can go ahead and create the image. The following command provides the name of the image and the tag. The last argument points to the context directory. A context directory contains the Dockerfile as well as any directories and files that are supposed to be included in the image. Here, the context directory is the current directory we reside in referenced by ".":

```
$ docker build -t java-hello-world:1.0.0 .
Sending build context to Docker daemon   8.32MB
Step 1/5 : FROM openjdk:11-jre-slim
 ---> 973c18dbf567
Step 2/5 : WORKDIR /app
 ---> Using cache
 ---> 31f9c5f2a019
Step 3/5 : COPY target/java-hello-world-0.0.1.jar java-hello-world.jar
 ---> Using cache
 ---> 6a1deee17e9d
Step 4/5 : ENTRYPOINT ["java", "-jar", "/app/java-hello-world.jar"]
 ---> Using cache
 ---> 52a91ca70d86
Step 5/5 : EXPOSE 8080
 ---> Using cache
 ---> 3e9c22451a17
Successfully built 3e9c22451a17
Successfully tagged java-hello-world:1.0.0
```

As indicated by the terminal output, the image has been created. You might have noticed that the base image has been downloaded as part of the process. Both images can be found in your local Docker Engine environment by running the following command:

```
$ docker images
REPOSITORY          TAG           IMAGE ID       CREATED             SIZE
java-hello-world    1.0.0         3e9c22451a17   About a minute ago  213MB
openjdk             11-jre-slim   973c18dbf567   20 hours ago        204MB
```

It's time to run the application in a container. The run command points to an image and executes its logic in a container:

```
$ docker run -d -p 8080:8080 java-hello-world:1.0.0
b0ee04accf078ea7c73cfe3be0f9d1ac6a099ac4e0e903773bc6bf6258acbb66
```

We told the command to forward the port 8080 accessible on localhost to the container port 8080. This means we should now be able to resolve the application's endpoint from the local machine. As you can see in the following command, a simple curl to the root context path renders the message "Hello World!":

```
$ curl localhost:8080
Hello World!
```

To publish an image to a registry, you'll potentially have to do some prework. Most registries require you to provide a prefix that signifies the username or hostname as part of the image name. For example, Docker Hub requires you to provide the username. My username is bmuschko and therefore I have to retag my image before pushing it. If the registry is protected, you'll also have to provide the credentials. For Docker Hub, we are logging in with username:

```
$ docker login --username=bmuschko
Password: *****
WARNING! Your password will be stored unencrypted in /Users/bmuschko/
.docker/config.json.
Configure a credential helper to remove this warning. See
https://docs.docker.com/engine/reference/commandline/login/#credentials-store

Login Succeeded
$ docker tag java-hello-world:1.0.0 bmuschko/java-hello-world:1.0.0
$ docker push bmuschko/java-hello-world:1.0.0
The push refers to repository [docker.io/bmuschko/java-hello-world]
be6f48684f94: Pushed
ff3b0a3f736e: Pushed
a346421f0657: Mounted from library/openjdk
cab8f1f311d9: Mounted from library/openjdk
0a71386e5425: Mounted from library/openjdk
ffc9b21953f4: Mounted from library/openjdk
1.0.0: digest: sha256:aafd2ab53ba3ff66fe66d7ffc118c7a8ea993472132d1bdf417a \
62e212f3dcfd size: 1578
```

You experienced one of the most common developer workflows: containerizing an application and pushing the image to a registry. There's far more to learn about Docker, but that is outside the scope of this book and we won't dive any deeper here. Refer to the Docker documentation (*https://docs.docker.com*) for more information.

Creating Pods

In this chapter, we will only look at the creation of a Pod running a single container. Jump right over to the Chapter 4, *Multi-Container Pods*, if you want to learn more about Pods that run more than one container. That chapter explains applicable design patterns and how to interact with individual containers using kubectl.

The Pod definition needs to state an image for every container. Upon creating the Pod object, imperatively or declaratively, the container runtime engine (CRI) will check if the container image already exists locally. If the image doesn't exist yet, the CRI will download it from a container image registry. By default the registry is

Docker Hub. As soon as the image exists on the node, the container is instantiated and run. Figure 2-5 demonstrates the execution flow on a high-level.

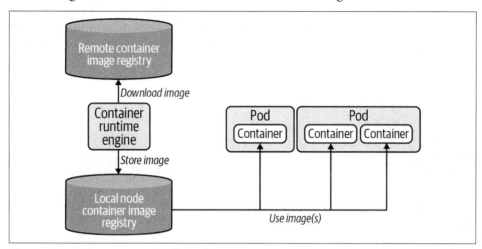

Figure 2-5. CRI interaction with Docker images

The run command is the central entry point for creating Pods imperatively. Let's talk about its usage and the most important command line options you should memorize and practice. Say you wanted to run a Hazelcast instance (*https://hazelcast.com*) inside of a Pod. The container should use the latest Hazelcast image (*https://oreil.ly/ChxPI*), expose port 5701, and define an environment variable. In addition, we'll also want to assign two labels to the Pod. The following command combines of this information and does not require any further editing of the live object:

```
$ kubectl run hazelcast --image=hazelcast/hazelcast --restart=Never \
  --port=5701 --env="DNS_DOMAIN=cluster" --labels="app=hazelcast,env=prod"
```

The run command offers a wealth of command line options. Execute the kubectl run --help or refer to the Kubernetes documentation for a broad overview. For the CKAD exam, you'll not need to understand each and every command. Table 2-1 lists the most commonly-used options.

Table 2-1. Important kubectl run command line options

Option	Example value	Description
--image	nginx	The image for the container to run.
--port	8080	The port that this container exposes.
--rm	-	Deletes the Pod after command in the container finishes.
--env	PROFILE=dev	The environment variables to set in the container.
--labels	app=frontend	A comma-separated list of labels to apply to the Pod.

Some developers are more used to the creation of Pods from a YAML manifest. Probably you're already accustomed to the declarative approach because you're using it at work. You can express the same configuration for the Hazelcast Pod by opening the editor, copying a Pod YAML code snippet from the Kubernetes online documentation and modifying it to your needs. Example 2-2 shows the Pod manifest saved in the file pod.yaml.

Example 2-2. Pod YAML manifest

```
apiVersion: v1
kind: Pod
metadata:
  name: hazelcast
  labels:
    app: hazelcast
    env: prod
spec:
  containers:
  - env:
    - name: DNS_DOMAIN
      value: cluster
    image: hazelcast/hazelcast
    name: hazelcast
    ports:
    - containerPort: 5701
  restartPolicy: Never
```

Creating the Pod from the manifest is straightforward. Simply use the create or apply command, as explained in the sections "Object Management" and "Other Notable Commands":

```
$ kubectl create -f pod.yaml
pod/hazelcast created
```

Listing Pods

Now that you created a Pod, you can further inspect its runtime information. The kubectl command offers a command for listing all Pods running in the cluster: get pods. The following command renders the Pod named hazelcast:

```
$ kubectl get pods
NAME        READY   STATUS    RESTARTS   AGE
hazelcast   1/1     Running   0          17s
```

Real-world Kubernetes clusters can run hundreds of Pods at the same time (*https://oreil.ly/I0Ckf*). If you know the name of the Pod of interest, it's often times easier to query by name. We would still only see a single Pod:

```
$ kubectl get pods hazelcast
NAME        READY   STATUS    RESTARTS   AGE
hazelcast   1/1     Running   0          17s
```

Pod Life Cycle Phases

Because Kubernetes is a state engine with asynchronous control loops, it's possible that the status of the Pod doesn't show a `Running` status right away when listing the Pods. It usually takes a couple of seconds to retrieve the image and start the container. Upon Pod creation, the object goes through several life cycle phases (*https://oreil.ly/Qk5Ob*), as shown in Figure 2-6.

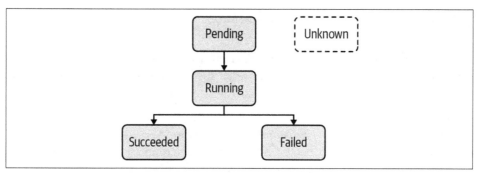

Figure 2-6. Pod Life cycle Phases

Understanding the implications of each phase is important as it gives you an idea about the operational status of a Pod. For example, during the exam you may be asked to identify a Pod with an issue and further debug the object. Table 2-2 describes all Pod life cycle phases.

Table 2-2. Pod life cycle phases

Option	Description
Pending	The Pod has been accepted by the Kubernetes system, but one or more of the container images has not been created.
Running	At least one container is still running, or is in the process of starting or restarting.
Succeeded	All containers in the Pod terminated successfully.
Failed	Containers in the Pod terminated, as least one failed with an error.
Unknown	The state of Pod could not be obtained.

Rendering Pod Details

The rendered table produced by the `get` command provides high-level information about a Pod. But what if you needed to have a deeper look at the details? The `describe` command can help:

```
$ kubectl describe pods hazelcast
Name:               hazelcast
Namespace:          default
Priority:           0
PriorityClassName:  <none>
Node:               docker-desktop/192.168.65.3
Start Time:         Wed, 20 May 2020 19:35:47 -0600
Labels:             app=hazelcast
                    env=prod
Annotations:        <none>
Status:             Running
IP:                 10.1.0.41
Containers:
  ...
Events:
  ...
```

The terminal output contains the metadata information of a Pod, the containers it runs and the event log, such as failures when the Pod was scheduled. The example output above has been condensed to just show the metadata section. You can expect the output to be very lengthy.

There's a way to be more specific about the information you want to render. You can combine the describe command with a Unix grep command. Say you wanted to identify the image for running in the container:

```
$ kubectl describe pods hazelcast | grep Image:
    Image:          hazelcast/hazelcast
```

Accessing Logs of a Pod

As application developers, we know very well what to expect in the log files produced by the application we implemented. Runtime failures may occur when operating an application in a container. The logs command downloads the log output of a container. The following output indicates that the Hazelcast server started up successfully:

```
$ kubectl logs hazelcast
...
May 25, 2020 3:36:26 PM com.hazelcast.core.LifecycleService
INFO: [10.1.0.46]:5701 [dev] [4.0.1] [10.1.0.46]:5701 is STARTED
```

It's very likely that more log entries will be produced as soon as the container receives traffic from end users. You can stream the logs with the command line option -f. This option is helpful if you want to see logs in real time.

Kubernetes tries to restart a container under certain conditions, such as if the image cannot be resolved on the first try. Upon a container restart, you'll not have access to the logs of the previous container anymore; the logs command only renders the logs for the current container. However, you can still get back to the logs of the previous container by adding the -p command line option. You may want to use the option to identify the root cause that triggered a container restart.

Executing a Command in Container

There are situations that require you to log into the container and explore the file system. Maybe you want to inspect the configuration of your application or debug the current state of your application. You can use the exec command to open a shell in the container to explore it interactively, as follows:

```
$ kubectl exec -it hazelcast -- /bin/sh
# ...
```

Notice that you do not have to provide the resource type. This command only works for a Pod. The two dashes (--) separate the exec command and its options from the command you want to run inside of the container.

It's also possible to just execute a single command inside of a container. Say you wanted to render the environment variables available to containers without having to be logged in. Just remove the interactive flag -it and provide the relevant command after the two dashes:

```
$ kubectl exec hazelcast -- env
...
DNS_DOMAIN=cluster
```

Deleting a Pod

Sooner or later you'll want to delete a Pod. During the exam, you may be asked to remove a Pod. Or possibly, you made a configuration mistake and want to start the question from scratch:

```
$ kubectl delete pod hazelcast
pod "hazelcast" deleted
```

Keep in mind that Kubernetes tries to delete a Pod *gracefully*. This means that the Pod will try to finish active requests to the Pod to avoid unnecessary disruption to the end user. A graceful deletion operation can take anywhere from 5-30 seconds, time you don't want to waste during the exam. See Chapter 1 for more information on how to speed up the process.

An alternative way to delete a Pod is to point the delete command to the YAML manifest you used to create it. The behavior is the same:

```
$ kubectl delete -f pod.yaml
pod "hazelcast" deleted
```

Configuring Pods

The CKAD curriculum expects you to feel comfortable with editing YAML manifests either as files or as live object representations. In this section, I want to point you to some of the typical configuration scenarios you may face during the exam. Later chapters will deepen your knowledge by touching on other configuration aspects.

Declaring Environment Variables

Applications need to expose a way to make their runtime behavior configurable. For example, you may want to inject the URL to an external web service or declare the username for a database connection. Environment variables are a common option to provide this runtime configuration.

Avoid creating container images per environment

It might be tempting to say "hey, let's create a container image for any target deployment environment I need including its configuration." That's a bad idea. One of the practices of continuous delivery (*https://oreil.ly/w4_2g*) and the Twelve-Factor App principles (*https://12factor.net*) is to only build a deployable artifact for a commit once. In this case, the artifact is the container image. Deviating configuration runtime behavior should be controllable by injecting runtime information when instantiating the container. You can use environment variables to control the behavior as needed.

Defining environment variables in a Pod YAML manifest is relatively easy. Add or enhance the section env of a container. Every environment variable consists of a key-value pair, represented by the attributes name and value. Kubernetes does not enforce or sanitize typical naming conventions for environment variable keys. It's recommended to follow the standard of using upper-case letters and the underscore character (_) to separate words.

To illustrate a set of environment variables, have a look at Example 2-3. The code snippet describes a Pod that runs a Java-based application using the Spring Boot framework.

Example 2-3. YAML manifest for a Pod defining environment variables

```
apiVersion: v1
kind: Pod
metadata:
  name: spring-boot-app
spec:
  containers:
```

```
- image: bmuschko/spring-boot-app:1.5.3
  name: spring-boot-app
  env:
  - name: SPRING_PROFILES_ACTIVE
    value: prod
  - name: VERSION
    value: '1.5.3'
```

The first environment variable named `SPRING_PROFILES_ACTIVE` defines a pointer to a so-called profile. A profile contains environment-specific properties. Here, we are pointing to the profile that configures the production environment. The environment variable `VERSION` specifies the application version. Its value corresponds to the tag of the image and can be exposed by the running application to display the value in the user interface.

Defining a Command with Arguments

Many container images already define an `ENTRYPOINT` or `CMD` instruction. The command assigned to the instruction is automatically executed as part of the container startup process. For example, the Hazelcast image we used earlier defines the instruction `CMD ["/opt/hazelcast/start-hazelcast.sh"]`.

In a Pod definition, you can either redefine the image `ENTRYPOINT` and `CMD` instructions or assign a command to execute for the container if hasn't been specified by the image. You can provide this information with the help of the `command` and `args` attributes for a container. The `command` attribute overrides the image's `ENTRYPOINT` instruction. The `args` attribute replaces the `CMD` instruction of an image.

Imagine you wanted to provide a command to an image that doesn't provide one yet. As usual there are two different approaches, imperatively and declaratively. We'll generate the YAML manifest with the help of the `run` command. The Pod should use the busybox image and execute a shell command that renders the current date every 10 seconds in an infinite loop:

```
$ kubectl run mypod --image=busybox -o yaml --dry-run=client --restart=Never \
  > pod.yaml -- /bin/sh -c "while true; do date; sleep 10; done"
```

You can see in the generated, but condensed `pod.yaml` file shown in Example 2-4 that the command has been turned into an `args` attribute. Kubernetes specifies each argument on a single line.

Example 2-4. A YAML manifest containing an args attribute

```
apiVersion: v1
kind: Pod
metadata:
  name: mypod
```

```
spec:
  containers:
  - args:
    - /bin/sh
    - -c
    - while true; do date; sleep 10; done
    image: busybox
    name: mypod
  restartPolicy: Never
```

You could have achieved the same by a combination of the `command` and `args` attributes if you were to hand-craft the YAML manifest. Example 2-5 shows the different approach.

Example 2-5. A YAML file containing command and args attributes

```
apiVersion: v1
kind: Pod
metadata:
  name: mypod
spec:
  containers:
  - command: ["/bin/sh"]
    args: ["-c", "while true; do date; sleep 10; done"]
    image: busybox
    name: mypod
  restartPolicy: Never
```

You can quickly verify if the declared command actually does its job. First, we create the Pod instance, then we tail the logs:

```
$ kubectl create -f pod.yaml
pod/mypod created
$ kubectl logs mypod -f
Fri May 29 00:49:06 UTC 2020
Fri May 29 00:49:16 UTC 2020
Fri May 29 00:49:26 UTC 2020
Fri May 29 00:49:36 UTC 2020
...
```

Understanding Namespaces

Namespaces are an API construct to avoid naming collisions and represent a scope for object names. A good use case for namespaces is to isolate the objects by team or responsibility. Most questions in the CKAD exam will ask you to execute the command in a specific namespace which has been set up for you. The following sections briefly touch on the basic operations needed to deal with a namespace.

Listing Namespaces

A Kubernetes cluster starts out with a couple of initial namespaces. You can list them with the following command:

```
$ kubectl get namespaces
NAME              STATUS    AGE
default           Active    157d
kube-node-lease   Active    157d
kube-public       Active    157d
kube-system       Active    157d
```

The default namespace hosts object that haven't been assigned to an explicit namespace. Namespaces starting with the prefix kube- are not considered end user-namespaces. They have been created by the Kubernetes system. You will not have to interact with them as an application developer.

Creating and Using a Namespace

To create a new namespace, use the create namespace command. The following command uses the name code-red:

```
$ kubectl create namespace code-red
namespace/code-red created
$ kubectl get namespace code-red
NAME       STATUS    AGE
code-red   Active    16s
```

The corresponding representation as a YAML manifest would look as follows:

```yaml
apiVersion: v1
kind: Namespace
metadata:
  name: code-red
```

Once the namespace is in place, you can create objects within it. You can do so with the command line option --namespace or its short-form -n. The following commands create a new Pod in the namespace code-red and then lists the available Pods in the namespace:

```
$ kubectl run pod --image=nginx --restart=Never -n code-red
pod/pod created
$ kubectl get pods -n code-red
NAME    READY    STATUS     RESTARTS    AGE
pod     1/1      Running    0           13s
```

Deleting a Namespace

Deleting a namespace has a cascading effect on the object existing in it. Deleting a namespace will automatically delete its objects:

```
$ kubectl delete namespace code-red
namespace "code-red" deleted
$ kubectl get pods -n code-red
No resources found in code-red namespace.
```

Summary

Kubernetes represents its functionality for deploying and operating a cloud-native application with the help of primitives. Each primitive follows a general structure: the API version, the kind, the metadata and the desired state of the resources, also called the spec. Upon creation or modification of the object, the Kubernetes scheduler automatically tries to ensure that the actual state of the object follows the defined specification. Every live object can be inspected, edited, and deleted.

The portion "Core Concepts" of the curriculum puts a strong emphasis on the concept of a Pod. The Pod is a Kubernetes primitive responsible for running an application in a container. Kubernetes uses Docker as its default container runtime technology. A Pod can define one or many containers that use a container image. Upon its creation, the container image is resolved and used to bootstrap the application. Every Pod can be further customized with the relevant YAML configuration.

Kubectl acts as a CLI-based client to interact with the Kubernetes cluster. You can use its commands and flags to manage Kubernetes objects.

Exam Essentials

Understand how to manage Kubernetes objects

In Kubernetes, you can create objects with the imperative or declarative approach. The imperative approach is the most time-efficient way to create objects. For Pods, use the command kubectl run, for any other resource use the command kubectl create. Furthermore, practice editing live objects with kubectl edit and know how to delete them via kubectl delete.

Know how to interact with Pods

A Pod runs an application inside of a container. You can check on the status and the configuration of the Pod by inspecting the object with the kubectl get or kubectl describe commands. Make yourself familiar with the life cycle phases of a Pod to be able to quickly diagnose error conditions. The command kubectl logs can be used to download the container log information without having to shell into the container. Use the command kubectl exec to further explore the container environment e.g. to check on processes or to examine files.

Advanced Pod configuration options

Sometimes you have to start with the YAML manifest of a Pod and then create the Pod declaratively. This could be the case if you wanted to provide environment variables to the container or declare a custom command. Practice different configuration options by copy-pasting relevant code snippets from the Kubernetes documentation.

Sample Exercises

Solutions to these exercises are available in the Appendix.

1. Create a new Pod named nginx running the image nginx:1.17.10. Expose the container port 80. The Pod should live in the namespace named ckad.

2. Get the details of the Pod including its IP address.

3. Create a temporary Pod that uses the busybox image to execute a wget command inside of the container. The wget command should access the endpoint exposed by the nginx container. You should see the HTML response body rendered in the terminal.

4. Get the logs of the nginx container.

5. Add the environment variables DB_URL=postgresql://mydb:5432 and DB_USER NAME=admin to the container of the nginx Pod.

6. Open a shell for the nginx container and inspect the contents of the current directory ls -l.

7. Create a YAML manifest for a Pod named loop that runs the busybox image in a container. The container should run the following command: for i in {1..10}; do echo "Welcome $i times"; done. Create the Pod from the YAML manifest. What's the status of the Pod?

8. Edit the Pod named loop. Change the command to run in an endless loop. Each iteration should echo the current date.

9. Inspect the events and the status of the Pod loop.

10. Delete the namespace ckad and its Pods.

## CHAPTER 3

Configuration

The domain "configuration" of the curriculum covers advanced concepts used to configure a Pod. This chapter will discuss all relevant Kubernetes primitives and their purpose with the help of a concrete use case.

As demonstrated in the previous chapter, controlling runtime behavior using environment variables is common practice. Having to deal with a long list of environment variables by defining them for individual containers can quickly become tedious, especially if you want to reuse some of those key-value pairs across a set of Pods. ConfigMaps and Secrets help with centralizing configuration data and can be injected into containers.

Furthermore, this chapter discusses security and resource consumption concerns. You can define a security context to define privilege and access control settings. Every namespace can limit the amount of resources like CPU and memory available to Pods. At the end of the chapter, you will understand how to create and inspect a ResourceQuota and how to set minimum and maximum resource boundaries for a Pod. Finally, we'll touch on the configuration needed to assign a Service Account to a Pod.

 This chapter will use the concept of a Volume. Reference Chapter 8 for more information if you're not familiar with Kubernetes' persistent storage options.

At a high level, this chapter covers the following concepts:

- ConfigMap
- Secret

- Volume
- Security Context
- Resource Boundaries
- ResourceQuota
- Service Account

Defining and Consuming Configuration Data

One of the fundamental principles of continuous delivery is to build a binary artifact just once for a single SCM commit. A binary artifact should then be stored in a binary repository—for example, in the commercial product JFrog Artifactory (*https://oreil.ly/e9IXy*). An automated process would then download the artifact if needed for deployment to a target environment. Typical target runtime environments include staging or production. The method of building an artifact just once prevents accidental mistakes if you were to rebuild it per environment and increases the overall confidence level when shipping the software to the customer. Configuration data needed for each of those environments can be injected into the runtime environment. Environment variables can help with this task, but there are other options.

Let's bridge the gap to container runtime environments like Docker. The same concept of building an artifact just once should apply here. In our case, the binary artifact is a container image. You will not want to rebuild the image for different runtime environments.

Kubernetes dedicates two primitives to defining configuration data: the ConfigMap and the Secret. Both primitives are completely decoupled from the lifecycle of a Pod, which enables you to change their configuration data values without necessarily having to redeploy the Pod. In essence, ConfigMaps and Secrets store a set of key-value pairs. Those key-value pairs can be injected into a container as environment variables, or they can be mounted as a Volume. Figure 3-1 shows an example Pod that decided to consume data from a ConfigMap as a volume mount and a Secret as environment variables.

What's the difference between a ConfigMap and a Secret? They're almost identical in purpose and structure, although Secrets are better suited for storing sensitive data like passwords, API keys, or SSL certificates because they store their values encoded in Base64. Let me also mention the security aspect of Secrets. Base64 only encodes a value, but it doesn't encrypt it. Therefore, anyone with access to its value can swiftly decode it. A Secret is distributed only to the nodes running Pods that actually require access to it. Moreover, Secrets are stored in memory and are never written to a physical storage.

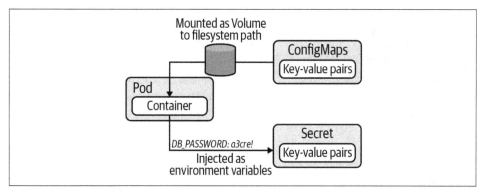

Figure 3-1. Consuming configuration data

Creating a ConfigMap

You can create a ConfigMap imperatively with a single command: `kubectl create configmap`. As part of the command, you have to provide a mandatory command-line flag that points to the source of the data. Kubernetes distinguishes four different options:

- Literal values, which are key-value pairs as plain text.
- A file that contains key-value pairs and expects them to be environment variables.
- A file with arbitrary contents.
- A directory with one or many files.

The following commands show all options in action. You will find that a file and directory use the same command-line option, `--from-file`. Later, we'll revisit how those key-value pairs are parsed and stored in a ConfigMap.

Literal values
```
$ kubectl create configmap db-config --from-literal=db=staging
configmap/db-config created
```

Single file with environment variables
```
$ kubectl create configmap db-config --from-env-file=config.env
configmap/db-config created
```

Single file
```
$ kubectl create configmap db-config --from-file=config.txt
configmap/db-config created
```

Directory containing files

```
$ kubectl create configmap db-config --from-file=app-config
configmap/db-config created
```

Alternatively, you can also create the ConfigMap declaratively. Say you decided to define key-value pairs as literal values; the YAML representation could look like what's shown in Example 3-1.

Example 3-1. ConfigMap YAML manifest

```
apiVersion: v1
kind: ConfigMap
metadata:
  name: backend-config
data:
  database_url: jdbc:postgresql://localhost/test
  user: fred
```

Consuming a ConfigMap as Environment Variables

Once the ConfigMap has been created, it can be consumed by one or many Pods in the same namespace. Here, we're exploring how to inject the key-value pairs of a ConfigMap as environment variables. The Pod definition shown in Example 3-2 references the ConfigMap named `backend-config` and injects the key-value pairs as environment variables with the help of `envFrom.configMapRef`.

Example 3-2. Injecting ConfigMap key-value pairs into the container

```
apiVersion: v1
kind: Pod
metadata:
  name: configured-pod
spec:
  containers:
  - image: nginx:1.19.0
    name: app
    envFrom:
    - configMapRef:
        name: backend-config
```

It's important to mention that the attribute `envFrom` does not automatically format the key to conform to typical conventions used by environment variables (all caps letters, words separated by the underscore character). The attribute simply uses the keys as-is. After creating the Pod, you can inspect the injected environment variables by executing the remote Unix command `env` inside of the container:

```
$ kubectl exec configured-pod -- env
...
database_url=jdbc:postgresql://localhost/test
user=fred
...
```

Sometimes, key-value pairs do not conform to typical naming conventions for environment variables or can't be changed without impacting running services. You can redefine the keys used to inject an environment variable into a Pod with the value From attribute. Example 3-3 turns the key database_url into DATABASE_URL and the key user into USERNAME.

Example 3-3. Reassigning environment variable keys for ConfigMap entries

```
apiVersion: v1
kind: Pod
metadata:
  name: configured-pod
spec:
  containers:
  - image: nginx:1.19.0
    name: app
    env:
    - name: DATABASE_URL
      valueFrom:
        configMapKeyRef:
          name: backend-config
          key: database_url
    - name: USERNAME
      valueFrom:
        configMapKeyRef:
          name: backend-config
          key: user
```

The resulting environment variables available to the container now follow the typical conventions for environment variables:

```
$ kubectl exec configured-pod -- env
...
DATABASE_URL=jdbc:postgresql://localhost/test
USERNAME=fred
...
```

Mounting a ConfigMap as Volume

Most programming languages can resolve and use environment variables to control the runtime behavior of an application. Especially when dealing with a long list of configuration data, it might be preferable to access the key-value pairs from the filesystem of the container.

A ConfigMap can be mounted as Volume. The application would then read those key-value pairs from the filesystem with an expected mount path. Kubernetes represents every key in the ConfigMap as a file. The value becomes the content of the file. Sound complicated? Let's have a look at Example 3-4.

Example 3-4. Mounting a ConfigMap as Volume

```
apiVersion: v1
kind: Pod
metadata:
  name: configured-pod
spec:
  containers:
  - image: nginx:1.19.0
    name: app
    volumeMounts:
    - name: config-volume
      mountPath: /etc/config
  volumes:
  - name: config-volume
    configMap:
      name: backend-config
```

In the YAML manifest shown in Example 3-4, I would like to point out the most important building blocks. The `volumes` attribute specifies the Volume to use. As you can see in the code snippet, it points to the name of the ConfigMap. The name of the Volume is relevant for adding the mount path using the `volumeMounts` attribute. Here, we're pointing to the mount path `/etc/config`.

To verify the expected behavior, open an interactive shell. As shown in the following terminal output, the directory contains the files *database_url* and *user*. Those filenames correspond to the keys of the ConfigMap. The file contents represent their corresponding value in the ConfigMap:

```
$ kubectl exec -it configured-pod -- /bin/sh
# ls -1 /etc/config
database_url
user
# cat /etc/config/database_url
jdbc:postgresql://localhost/test
# cat /etc/config/user
fred
```

Creating a Secret

You can create a Secret imperatively with a single command: `kubectl create secret`. Similar to the command for creating a ConfigMap, you will have to provide an additional subcommand and a configuration option. It's mandatory to spell out the subcommand right after the Kubernetes resource type `secret`. You can select from one of the options shown in Table 3-1.

Table 3-1. Options for creating a Secret

Option	Description
generic	Creates a secret from a file, directory, or literal value.
docker-registry	Creates a secret for use with a Docker registry.
tls	Creates a TLS secret.

In most cases, you will likely deal with the type `generic`, which provides the same command-line options to point to the source of the configuration data as `kubectl create configmap`:

- Literal values, which are key-value pairs as plain text.
- A file that contains key-value pairs and expects them to be environment variables.
- A file with arbitrary contents.
- A directory with one or many files.

Let's have a look at some command-line usage examples for creating a Secret with the type `generic`. All values you feed into the command will be stored internally Base64 encoded. For example, the value `s3cre!` turns into `czNjcmUh`.

Literal values

```
$ kubectl create secret generic db-creds --from-literal=pwd=s3cre!
secret/db-creds created
```

File containing environment variables

```
$ kubectl create secret generic db-creds --from-env-file=secret.env
secret/db-creds created
```

SSH key file

```
$ kubectl create secret generic ssh-key --from-file=id_rsa=~/.ssh/id_rsa
secret/db-creds created
```

Of course, you can always take the declarative route, but there's a little catch. You have to Base64-encode the configuration data value yourself when using the type `Opaque`. How can you do so? One way to encode and decode a value is the Unix command-line tool `base64`. Alternatively, you can use websites like Base64 Encode (*https:// oreil.ly/xIgbr*). The following example uses the command-line tool:

```
$ echo -n 's3cre!' | base64
czNjcmUh
```

You can now plug in the value under the data section with a corresponding key, as shown in Example 3-5.

Example 3-5. A Secret with Base64-encoded values

```
apiVersion: v1
kind: Secret
metadata:
  name: db-creds
type: Opaque
data:
  pwd: czNjcmUh
```

Refer to the Kubernetes documentation for other types assignable to a Secret (*https://oreil.ly/erPVn*) that do not require explicit Base64-encoding. One example is the type kubernetes.io/basic-auth, which represents credentials needed for basic authentication.

Consuming a Secret as Environment Variables

Consuming the key-value pairs of a Secret as environment variables from a container works almost exactly the same way as it does for a ConfigMap. There's only one difference: instead of using envFrom.configMapRef, you'd use envFrom.secretRef, as shown in Example 3-6.

Example 3-6. Injecting key-value pairs of a Secret into a container

```
apiVersion: v1
kind: Pod
metadata:
  name: configured-pod
spec:
  containers:
  - image: nginx:1.19.0
    name: app
    envFrom:
    - secretRef:
        name: db-creds
```

It's important to understand that the container will make the environment variable available in a Base64-decoded value. In turn, your application running in the container will not have to implement Base64-decoding logic:

```
$ kubectl exec configured-pod -- env
...
pwd=s3cre!
...
```

Mounting a Secret as Volume

In practice, you will see Secrets mounted as Volumes fairly often, especially in the context of making an SSH private key available to the container. Example 3-7 assumes you've created a Secret named `ssh-key` with the key `id_rsa`. First, create a Volume by pointing it to the name of the Secret with `secret.secretName`. Note that the attribute referencing the name is different than for a ConfigMap; for Secrets, it's called `secretName`. Next, mount the Volume by its name and provide a mount path.

Example 3-7. Mounting a Secret as Volume

```
apiVersion: v1
kind: Pod
metadata:
  name: configured-pod
spec:
  containers:
  - image: nginx:1.19.0
    name: app
    volumeMounts:
    - name: secret-volume
      mountPath: /var/app
      readOnly: true
  volumes:
  - name: secret-volume
    secret:
      secretName: ssh-key
```

Secrets mounted as Volume will expose its values in Base64-decoded form. You can easily verify the value by opening an interactive shell and printing the contents of the file */var/app/id_rsa* to standard output:

```
$ kubectl exec -it configured-pod -- /bin/sh
# ls -1 /var/app
id_rsa
# cat /var/app/id_rsa
-----BEGIN RSA PRIVATE KEY-----
Proc-Type: 4,ENCRYPTED
DEK-Info: AES-128-CBC,8734C9153079F2E8497C8075289EBBF1
...
-----END RSA PRIVATE KEY-----
```

Understanding Security Contexts

Docker images can define security-relevant instructions to reduce the attack vector for the running container. By default, containers run with root privileges, which provide supreme access to all processes and the container's filesystem. As a best practice, you should craft the corresponding Dockerfile in a such a way that the container will be run with a user ID other than 0 with the help of the USER instruction. There are many other ways to secure a container on the container level, but we won't go into any more detail here.

Kubernetes, as the container orchestration engine, can apply additional configuration to increase container security. You'd do so by defining a security context. A security context defines privilege and access control settings for a Pod or a container. The following list provides some examples:

- The user ID that should be used to run the Pod and/or container.
- The group ID that should be used for filesystem access.
- Granting a running process inside the container some privileges of the root user but not all of them.

The security context is not a Kubernetes primitive. It is modeled as a set of attributes under the directive securityContext within the Pod specification. Security settings defined on the Pod level apply to all containers running in the Pod; however, container-level settings take precedence. For more information on Pod-level security attributes, see the PodSecurityContext (*https://oreil.ly/EUL2-*) API. Container-level security attributes can be found in the SecurityContext (*https://oreil.ly/EfUg5*) API.

To make the functionality more transparent, let's have a look at a use case. Some images, like the one for the open source reverse-proxy server NGINX (*https://oreil.ly/kYjux*), must be run with the root user. Say you wanted to enforce that containers cannot be run as a root user as a sensible security strategy. The YAML manifest shown in Example 3-8 defines the security configuration specifically to a container. If you were to run other containers inside the Pod, then the runAsNonRoot setting would not have any effect on them.

Example 3-8. Setting a security context on the container level

```
apiVersion: v1
kind: Pod
metadata:
  name: non-root
spec:
  containers:
  - image: nginx:1.18.0
    name: secured-container
    securityContext:
      runAsNonRoot: true
```

You will see that Kubernetes does its job; however, the image is not compatible. Therefore, the container fails during the startup process with the status Create ContainerConfigError:

```
$ kubectl create -f container-root-user.yaml
pod/non-root created
$ kubectl get pods
NAME        READY   STATUS                            RESTARTS   AGE
non-root    0/1     CreateContainerConfigError        0          7s
$ kubectl describe pod/non-root
...
Events:
Type      Reason      Age                 From                Message
----      ------      ----                ----                -------
Normal    Scheduled   <unknown>           default-scheduler   Successfully assigned \
                                                              default/non-root to minikube
Normal    Pulling     18s                 kubelet, minikube   Pulling image "nginx:1.18.0"
Normal    Pulled      14s                 kubelet, minikube   Successfully pulled image \
                                                              "nginx:1.18.0"
Warning   Failed      0s (x3 over 14s)    kubelet, minikube   Error: container has \
                                                              runAsNonRoot and image \
                                                              will run as root
```

There are alternative NGINX images available that are not required to run with the root user. One example is bitnami/nginx (*https://oreil.ly/bBhBf*). Upon a closer look at the Dockerfile that produced the image, you will find that the container runs with the user ID 1001. Starting the container with the runAsNonRoot directive will work just fine.

There are many other security restrictions you can impose on a container running in Kubernetes. For example, you may want to set the access control for files and directories. Say that, whenever a file is created on the filesystem, the owner of the file should be the arbitrary group ID 3500. The YAML manifest shown in Example 3-9 assigns the security context settings on the Pod level as a direct child of the spec attribute.

Example 3-9. Setting a security context on the Pod level

```
apiVersion: v1
kind: Pod
metadata:
  name: fs-secured
spec:
  securityContext:
    fsGroup: 3500
  containers:
  - image: nginx:1.18.0
    name: secured-container
    volumeMounts:
    - name: data-volume
      mountPath: /data/app
  volumes:
  - name: data-volume
    emptyDir: {}
```

You can easily verify the effect of setting the filesystem group ID. Open an interactive shell to the container, navigate to the mounted Volume, and create a new file. Inspecting the ownership of the file will show the group ID 3500 automatically assigned to it:

```
$ kubectl create -f pod-file-system-group.yaml
pod/fs-secured created
$ kubectl get pods
NAME            READY    STATUS     RESTARTS    AGE
fs-secured      1/1      Running    0           24s
$ kubectl exec -it fs-secured -- /bin/sh
# cd /data/app
# touch logs.txt
# ls -l
-rw-r--r-- 1 root 3500 0 Jul  9 01:41 logs.txt
```

Understanding Resource Boundaries

Namespaces do not enforce any quotas for computing resources like CPU, memory, or disk space, nor do they limit the number of Kubernetes objects that can be created. As a result, Kubernetes objects can consume unlimited resources until the maximum available capacity is reached. In a cloud environment, resources are provisioned on demand as long as you pay the bill. I think we can agree that that approach doesn't scale well.

 Kubernetes measures CPU resources in millicores and memory resources in bytes. That's why you might see resources defined as 600m or 100Mib. For a deep dive on those resource units, it's worth cross-referencing the section "Resource units in Kubernetes" (*https://oreil.ly/ZaTCX*) in the official documentation.

Creating a ResourceQuota

The Kubernetes primitive ResourceQuota establishes the usable, maximum amount of resources per namespace. Once put in place, the Kubernetes scheduler will take care of enforcing those rules. The following list should give you an idea of the rules that can be defined:

- Setting an upper limit for the number of objects that can be created for a specific type (e.g., a maximum of 3 Pods).
- Limiting the total sum of compute resources (e.g., 3 GiB of RAM).
- Expecting a Quality of Service (QoS) class for a Pod (e.g., BestEffort to indicate that the Pod must not make any memory or CPU limits or requests).

Creating a ResourceQuota object is usually a task a Kubernetes administrator would take on, but it's relatively easy to define and create such an object. First, create the namespace the quota should apply to:

```
$ kubectl create namespace team-awesome
namespace/team-awesome created
$ kubectl get namespace
NAME            STATUS   AGE
team-awesome    Active   23s
```

Next, define the ResourceQuota in YAML. To demonstrate the functionality of a ResourceQuota, add constraints to the namespace, as shown in Example 3-10:

- Limit the number of Pods to 2.

- Define the minimum resources requested by a Pod to 1 CPU and 1024m of RAM.

- Define the maximum resources used by a Pod to 4 CPUs and 4096m of RAM.

Example 3-10. Defining hard resource limits with ResourceQuota

```
apiVersion: v1
kind: ResourceQuota
metadata:
  name: awesome-quota
spec:
  hard:
    pods: 2
    requests.cpu: "1"
    requests.memory: 1024m
    limits.cpu: "4"
    limits.memory: 4096m
```

You're ready to create a ResourceQuota for the namespace. After it's created, the object provides a convenient table overview for comparing used resources with the hard limits set by the ResourceQuota spec via the `describe` command:

```
$ kubectl create -f awesome-quota.yaml --namespace=team-awesome
resourcequota/awesome-quota created
$ kubectl describe resourcequota awesome-quota --namespace=team-awesome
Name:            awesome-quota
Namespace:       team-awesome
Resource         Used  Hard
--------         ----  ----
limits.cpu       0     4
limits.memory    0     4096m
pods             0     2
requests.cpu     0     1
requests.memory  0     1024m
```

Exploring ResourceQuota Enforcement

With the quota rules in place for the namespace `team-awesome`, we'll want to see its enforcement in action. We'll start by creating more than the maximum number of Pods, which is two. To test this, we can create Pods with any definition we like. Say, for example, we use a bare-bones definition that runs the image `nginx:1.18.0` in the container, as shown in Example 3-11.

Example 3-11. A Pod without resource requirements

```
apiVersion: v1
kind: Pod
metadata:
  name: nginx
spec:
  containers:
  - image: nginx:1.18.0
    name: nginx
```

From that YAML definition, let's create a Pod and see what happens. In fact, Kubernetes will reject the creation of the object with the following error message:

```
$ kubectl create -f nginx-pod.yaml --namespace=team-awesome
Error from server (Forbidden): error when creating "nginx-pod.yaml": \
pods "nginx" is forbidden: failed quota: awesome-quota: must specify \
limits.cpu,limits.memory,requests.cpu,requests.memory
```

Because we defined minimum and maximum resource requirements for objects in the namespace, we'll have to ensure that the YAML manifest actually defines them. Modify the initial definition by updating the instruction under `resources`, as shown in Example 3-12.

Example 3-12. A Pod with resource requirements

```
apiVersion: v1
kind: Pod
metadata:
  name: nginx
spec:
  containers:
  - image: nginx:1.18.0
    name: nginx
    resources:
      requests:
        cpu: "0.5"
        memory: "512m"
      limits:
        cpu: "1"
        memory: "1024m"
```

We should be able to create two uniquely named Pods with that manifest, as the combined resource requirements still fit with the boundaries defined in the ResourceQuota:

```
$ kubectl create -f nginx-pod1.yaml --namespace=team-awesome
pod/nginx1 created
$ kubectl create -f nginx-pod2.yaml --namespace=team-awesome
pod/nginx2 created
$ kubectl describe resourcequota awesome-quota --namespace=team-awesome
Name:             awesome-quota
Namespace:        team-awesome
Resource          Used    Hard
--------          ----    ----
limits.cpu        2       4
limits.memory     2048m   4096m
pods              2       2
requests.cpu      1       1
requests.memory   1024m   1024m
```

You may be able to imagine what would happen if we tried to create another Pod with the definition of nginx1 and nginx2. It will fail for two reasons. For one, we're not allowed to create a third Pod in the namespace, as the maximum number is set to two. Moreover, we'd exceed the alotted maximum for requests.cpu and requests.memory. The following error message provides us with this information:

```
$ kubectl create -f nginx-pod3.yaml --namespace=team-awesome
Error from server (Forbidden): error when creating "nginx-pod3.yaml": \
pods "nginx3" is forbidden: exceeded quota: awesome-quota, requested: \
pods=1,requests.cpu=500m,requests.memory=512m, used: pods=2,requests.cpu=1, \
requests.memory=1024m, limited: pods=2,requests.cpu=1,requests.memory=1024m
```

Understanding Service Accounts

We've been using the kubectl executable to run operations against a Kubernetes cluster. Under the hood, its implementation calls the API server by making an HTTP call to the exposed endpoints. Some applications running inside of a Pod may have to communicate with the API server as well. For example, the application may ask for specific cluster node information or available namespaces.

Pods use a Service Account to authenticate with the API server through an authentication token. A Kubernetes administrator assigns rules to a Service Account via role-based access control (RBAC) to authorize access to specific resources and actions. We won't go deeper into the concepts of RBAC, as the CKAD curriculum doesn't cover the topic. You can read more about it in the Kubernetes documentation (*https://oreil.ly/MOZ_X*). Figure 3-2 shows a high-level overview:

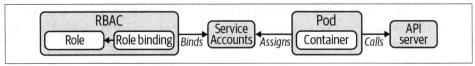

Figure 3-2. Using a Service Account to communicate with an API server

So far, we haven't defined a Service Account for a Pod. If not assigned explicitly, a Pod uses the `default` Service Account. The `default` Service Account has the same permissions as an unauthenticated user. This means that the Pod cannot view or modify the cluster state nor list or modify any of its resources.

You can query for the available Service Accounts with the subcommand `serviceaccounts`. You should only see the default Service Account listed:

```
$ kubectl get serviceaccounts
NAME      SECRETS   AGE
default   1         25d
```

Kubernetes models the authentication token with the Secret primitive. It's easy to identify the corresponding Secret for a Service Account. Retrieve the YAML representation of the Service Account and look at the attribute `secrets`. In the Secret, you can find the Base64-encoded values of the current namespace, the cluster certificate, and the authentication token:

```
$ kubectl get serviceaccount default -o yaml | grep -A 1 secrets:
secrets:
- name: default-token-bf8rh
$ kubectl get secret default-token-bf8rh -o yaml
apiVersion: v1
data:
  ca.crt: LS0tLS1CRUdJTiB...0FURS0tLS0tCg==
  namespace: ZGVmYXVsdA==
  token: ZXlKaGGJHY2lPaUp...ThzU0pooeFMxR013
kind: Secret
...
```

You will find that any live Pod object indicates its assigned Service Account in the spec section. The following command renders the value in the terminal:

```
$ kubectl run nginx --image=nginx --restart=Never
pod/nginx created
$ kubectl get pod nginx -o yaml
apiVersion: v1
kind: Pod
metadata:
  ...
spec:
  serviceAccountName: default
...
```

Creating and Assigning Custom Service Accounts

It's very possible that you'll want to grant certain permissions to an application running in a Pod. For that purpose, you'd create a custom Service Account and bind the relevant permissions to it. For the most part, this is the job of a Kubernetes administrator; however, it's good to have a basic understanding of the process from the perspective of an application developer.

To create a new Service Account, you can simply use the `create` command:

```
$ kubectl create serviceaccount custom
serviceaccount/custom created
```

Now, there are two ways to assign the Service Account to a Pod. You can either edit the YAML manifest and add the `serviceAccountName` attribute as shown above, or you can use the `--serviceaccount` flag in conjunction with the `run` command when creating the Pod:

```
$ kubectl run nginx --image=nginx --restart=Never --serviceaccount=custom
pod/nginx created
$ kubectl get pod nginx -o yaml
apiVersion: v1
kind: Pod
metadata:
  ...
spec:
  serviceAccountName: custom
...
```

Summary

Kubernetes provides advanced configuration options for Pods and containers. Many of those options are represented as primitives, and others simply blend in with the YAML configuration from the previous chapter. This chapter covered the topics ConfigMaps, Secrets, Security Contexts, resource requirements, and Service Accounts, all of which are important concepts to application developers aiming to operate secure, maintainable, and right-sized cloud native applications.

Coupling configuration to a container image can easily become a maintenence nightmare. Instead of hardcoding environment variables or embedding configuration files as instructions when building the image, it's much easier to inject this information when starting the container. In Kubernetes, this functionality is covered by the primitives ConfigMaps and Secrets. Both concepts define decoupled configuration data that can be injected into Pods as environment variables or mounted as Volume. ConfigMaps contain key-value pairs as plain-text tuples. This primitive is a good fit for nonsensitive, unencrypted configuration information like connection URLs to other microservices or usernames. Secrets build on the foundation of ConfigMaps but are meant for storing sensitive data like passwords or API keys. The manifest for a Secret looks pretty similar to the one for a ConfigMap; however, all values in the `data` section are Base64 encoded. Remember that Base64 encoding is not an encyrption mechanism—everyone who has access to the value can easily decode it. Therefore, you will not want to check in a Secret as code into a version control repository.

By default, containers run with the privileges of a `root` user. That means full access to the filesystem and the ability to run any process, opening up the possibility of security breaches by malicious attackers. You can counteract that risk by defining a security context for a Pod or container. For example, you could specify that the container can only be run as a non-root user. It's important to remember that the container-level definition takes precedence over the Pod-level security context.

A ResourceQuota defines the computing resources (e.g., CPU, RAM, and disk space) available to a namespace to prevent unbounded consumption by Pods running it. You can also limit the number of resource types that are allowed to be created. Accordingly, Pods have to work within those resource boundaries by declaring their minimum and maximum resource expectations. The Kubernetes scheduler will enforce those boundaries upon object creation.

Lastly, the Service Account defines the permissions for a Pod that needs to communicate with the API server. Every Pod uses a Service Account. If none is defined, Kubernetes will automatically assign the `default` Service Account. The `default` Service Account uses the privileges of an unauthenticated user. You can create a custom Service Account to allow for more fine-grained control. Assigning a custom Service Account to a Pod is as easy as defining it with `spec.serviceAccountName`.

Exam Essentials

Know how to create and consume ConfigMaps and Secrets

It's important to understand the intricate differences between the two primitives and practice how to create those objects imperatively and declaratively. The fastest way to create the objects is by using the `create configmap` and `create secret` commands. While assigning literal key-value pairs is straightforward, pointing to files and directories as data sources comes with subtle implications. Become familiar with the way Kubernetes references the information in the manifest. As a cross-check, inspect the configuration data for correctness by shelling into the container for both scenarios: injected as environment variables and mounted as Volume. Remember that you only need to provide a Base64-encoded value when creating a Secret from a YAML manifest. The imperative creation process performs the conversion automatically.

Experiment with options available to security contexts

The Kubernetes user documentation and API documentation is a good starting point for exploring security context options. You will find that there's an overlap in the options available to a PodSecurityContext and a SecurityContext. If defined on the Pod level, those options can be overridden by specifying them with a different value on the container level. While working through the different use cases solved by a security context option, verify their outcome by running an operation that should either be permitted or disallowed.

Understand resource boundaries

A ResourceQuota defines the resource boundaries for objects living within a namespace. The most commonly used boundaries apply to computing resources. Practice defining them and understand their effect on the creation of Pods. It's important to know the command for listing the hard requirements of a ResourceQuota and the resources currently in use. You will find that a ResourceQuota offers other options. Discover them in more detail for a broader exposure to the topic.

Know how to create and assign a custom Service Account

Application developers don't have to create custom Service Accounts on a day-to-day basis—that's the job of a Kubernetes administrator. Nevertheless, it's helpful to understand the background of Service Accounts and how this concept ties into RBAC. For the exam, practice the creation of a Service Account and know how to assign it to a Pod. You will not need to understand the RBAC aspect, as it is out of scope of the exam.

Sample Exercises

Solutions to these exercises are available in the Appendix.

1. Create a directory with the name *config*. Within the directory, create two files. The first file should be named *db.txt* and contain the key-value pair `password=mypwd`. The second file is named *ext-service.txt* and should define the key-value pair `api_key=LmLHbYhsgWZwNifiqaRorH8T`.

2. Create a Secret named `ext-service-secret` that uses the directory as data source and inspect the YAML representation of the object.

3. Create a Pod named `consumer` with the image `nginx` and mount the Secret as a Volume with the mount path */var/app*. Open an interactive shell and inspect the values of the Secret.

4. Use the declarative approach to create a ConfigMap named `ext-service-configmap`. Feed in the key-value pairs `api_endpoint=https://myapp.com/api` and `username=bot` as literals.

5. Inject the ConfigMap values into the existing Pod as environment variables. Ensure that the keys conform to typical naming conventions of environment variables.

6. Open an interactive shell and inspect the values of the ConfigMap.

7. Define a security context on the container level of a new Pod named `security-context-demo` that uses the image `alpine`. The security context adds the Linux capability `CAP_SYS_TIME` to the container. Explain if the value of this security context can be redefined in a Pod-level security context.

8. Define a ResourceQuota for the namespace `project-firebird`. The rules should constrain the count of Secret objects within the namespace to 1.

9. Create as many Secret objects within the namespace until the maximum number enforced by the ResourceQuota has been reached.

10. Create a new Service Account named `monitoring` and assign it to a new Pod with an image of your choosing. Open an interactive shell and locate the authentication token of the assigned Service Account.

## CHAPTER 4

Multi-Container Pods

The previous chapters explained how to manage single-container Pods. That's the norm, as you'll want to run a microservice inside of a single Pod to reinforce separation of concerns and increased cohesion. Technically, a Pod allows you to configure and run multiple containers. The section "Multi-Container Pods" of the CKAD curriculum addresses this concern.

In this chapter, we'll discuss the need for multi-container Pods, their relevant use cases, and the design patterns that emerged in the Kubernetes community. The exam outline specifically mentions three design patterns: the sidecar, the adapter, and the ambassador. We'll make sure to get a good grasp of their application with the help of representative examples.

We'll also talk about init containers. Init containers help with transitioning the runtime environment into an expected state so that the application can work properly. While it's not explicitly mentioned in the CKAD curriculum, I think it's important to cover the concept, as it falls under the topic of multi-container Pods.

At a high level, this chapter covers the following concepts:

- Pod
- Container
- Volume
- Design patterns

This chapter will use the concept of a Volume. Reference Chapter 8 for more information if you're not familiar with Kubernetes' persistent storage options.

Defining Multiple Containers in a Pod

Especially to beginners of Kubernetes, how to appropriately design a Pod isn't necessarily apparent. Upon reading the Kubernetes user documentation and tutorials on the internet, you'll quickly find out that you can create a Pod that runs multiple containers at the same time. The question often arises, "Should I deploy my microservices stack to a single Pod with multiple containers, or should I create multiple Pods, each running a single microservice?" The short answer is to operate a single microservice per Pod. This modus operandi promotes a decentralized, decoupled, and distributed architecture. Furthermore, it helps with rolling out new versions of a microservice without necessarily interrupting other parts of the system.

So what's the point of running multiple containers in a Pod then? There are two common use cases. Sometimes, you'll want to initialize your Pod by executing setup scripts, commands, or any other kind of preconfiguration procedure before the application container should start. This logic runs in a so-called init container. Other times, you'll want to provide helper functionality that runs alongside the application container to avoid the need to bake the logic into application code. For example, you may want to massage the log output produced by the application. Containers running helper logic are called *sidecars*.

Init Containers

Init containers provide initialization logic concerns to be run before the main application even starts. To draw an analogy, let's look at a similar concept in programming languages. Many programming languages, especially the ones that are object oriented like Java or C++, come with a constructor or a static method block. Those language constructs initialize fields, validate data, and set the stage before a class can be created. Not all classes need a constructor, but they are equipped with the capability.

In Kubernetes, this functionality can be achieved with the help of init containers. Init containers are always started before the main application containers, which means they have their own lifecycle. To split up the initialization logic, you can even distribute the work into multiple init containers that are run in the order of definition in the manifest. Of course, initialization logic can fail. If an init container produces an error, the whole Pod is restarted, causing all init containers to run again in sequential order. Thus, to prevent any side effects, making init container logic idempotent is a good practice. Figure 4-1 shows a Pod with two init containers and the main application.

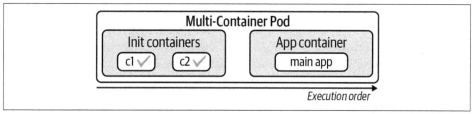

Figure 4-1. Sequential and atomic lifecycle of init containers in a Pod

In the past couple of chapters, we've explored how to define a container within a Pod. You simply specify its configuration under `spec.containers`. For init containers, Kubernetes provides a separate section: `spec.initContainers`. Init containers are always executed before the main application containers, regardless of the definition order in the manifest. The manifest shown in Example 4-1 defines an init container and a main application container. The init container sets up a configuration file in the directory */usr/shared/app*. This directory has been shared through a Volume so that it can be referenced by a Node.js-based application running in the main container.

Example 4-1. A Pod defining an init container

```
apiVersion: v1
kind: Pod
metadata:
  name: business-app
spec:
  initContainers:
  - name: configurer
    image: busybox:1.32.0
    command: ['sh', '-c', 'echo Configuring application... && \
              mkdir -p /usr/shared/app && echo -e "{\"dbConfig\": \
              {\"host\":\"localhost\",\"port\":5432,\"dbName\":\"customers\"}}" \
              > /usr/shared/app/config.json']
    volumeMounts:
    - name: configdir
      mountPath: "/usr/shared/app"
  containers:
  - image: bmuschko/nodejs-read-config:1.0.0
    name: web
    ports:
    - containerPort: 8080
    volumeMounts:
    - name: configdir
      mountPath: "/usr/shared/app"
  volumes:
  - name: configdir
    emptyDir: {}
```

When starting the Pod, you'll see that the status column of the `get` command provides information on init containers as well. The prefix `Init:` signifies that an init container is in the process of being executed. The status portion after the colon character shows the number of init containers completed versus the overall number of init containers configured:

```
$ kubectl create -f init.yaml
pod/business-app created
$ kubectl get pod business-app
NAME          READY   STATUS      RESTARTS   AGE
business-app  0/1     Init:0/1    0          2s
$ kubectl get pod business-app
NAME          READY   STATUS      RESTARTS   AGE
business-app  1/1     Running     0          8s
```

Errors can occur during the execution of init containers. You can always retrieve the logs of an init container by using the `--container` command-line option (or `-c` in its short form), as shown in Figure 4-2.

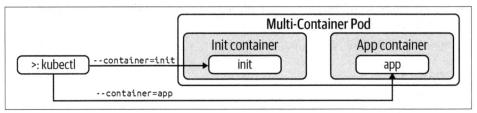

Figure 4-2. Targeting a specific container

The following command renders the logs of the `configurer` init container, which equates to the echo command we configured in the YAML manifest:

```
$ kubectl logs business-app -c configurer
Configuring application...
```

The Sidecar Pattern

The lifecycle of an init container looks as follows: it starts up, runs its logic, then terminates once the work has been done. Init containers are not meant to keep running over a longer period of time. There are scenarios that call for a different usage pattern. For example, you may want to create a Pod that runs multiple containers continuously alongside one another.

Typically, there are two different categories of containers: the container that runs the application and another container that provides helper functionality to the primary application. In the Kubernetes space, the container providing helper functionality is called a *sidecar*. Among the most commonly used capabilities of a sidecar container are file synchronization, logging, and watcher capabilities. The sidecars are not part of the main traffic or API of the primary application. They usually operate asynchronously and are not involved in the public API.

To illustrate the behavior of a sidecar, we'll consider the following use case. The main application container runs a web server—in this case, NGINX. Once started, the web server produces two standard logfiles. The file */var/log/nginx/access.log* captures requests to the web server's endpoint. The other file, */var/log/nginx/error.log*, records failures while processing incoming requests.

As part of the Pod's functionality, we'll want to implement a monitoring service. The sidecar container polls the file's *error.log* periodically and checks if any failures have been discovered. More specifically, the service tries to find failures assigned to the error log level, indicated by [error] in the log file. If an error is found, the monitoring service will react to it. For example, it could send a notification to the administrators of the system. We'll keep the functionality as simple as possible. The monitoring service will simply render an error message to standard output. The file exchange between the main application container and the sidecar container happens through a Volume, as shown in Figure 4-3.

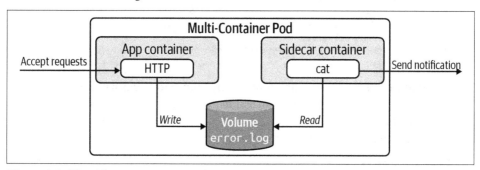

Figure 4-3. The sidecar pattern in action

The YAML manifest shown in Example 4-2 sets up the described scenario. The most tricky portion of the code is the lengthy bash command. The command runs an infinite loop. As part of each iteration, we inspect the contents of the file *error.log*, grep for an error and potentially act on it. The loop executes every 10 seconds.

Example 4-2. An exemplary sidecar pattern implementation

```
apiVersion: v1
kind: Pod
metadata:
  name: webserver
spec:
  containers:
  - name: nginx
    image: nginx
```

```
  volumeMounts:
  - name: logs-vol
    mountPath: /var/log/nginx
- name: sidecar
  image: busybox
  command: ["sh","-c","while true; do if [ \"$(cat /var/log/nginx/error.log \
            | grep 'error')\" != \"\" ]; then echo 'Error discovered!'; fi; \
            sleep 10; done"]
  volumeMounts:
  - name: logs-vol
    mountPath: /var/log/nginx
volumes:
- name: logs-vol
  emptyDir: {}
```

When starting up the Pod, you'll notice that the overall number of containers will show 2. After all containers can be started, the Pod signals a Running status:

```
$ kubectl create -f sidecar.yaml
pod/webserver created
$ kubectl get pods webserver
NAME         READY    STATUS               RESTARTS    AGE
webserver    0/2      ContainerCreating    0           4s
$ kubectl get pods webserver
NAME         READY    STATUS     RESTARTS    AGE
webserver    2/2      Running    0           5s
```

You will find that *error.log* does not contain any failure to begin with. It starts out as an empty file. With the following commands, you'll provoke an error on purpose. After waiting for at least 10 seconds, you'll find the expected message on the terminal, which you can query for with the logs command:

```
$ kubectl logs webserver -c sidecar
$ kubectl exec webserver -it -c sidecar -- /bin/sh
/ # wget -O- localhost?unknown
Connecting to localhost (127.0.0.1:80)
wget: server returned error: HTTP/1.1 404 Not Found
/ # cat /var/log/nginx/error.log
2020/07/18 17:26:46 [error] 29#29: *2 open() "/usr/share/nginx/html/unknown" \
failed (2: No such file or directory), client: 127.0.0.1, server: localhost, \
request: "GET /unknown HTTP/1.1", host: "localhost"
/ # exit
$ kubectl logs webserver -c sidecar
Error discovered!
```

The Adapter Pattern

As application developers, we want to focus on implementing business logic. For example, as part of a two-week sprint, say we're tasked with adding a shopping cart feature. In addition to the functional requirements, we also have to think about operational aspects like exposing administrative endpoints or crafting meaningful and properly formatted log output. It's easy to fall into the habit of simply rolling all aspects into the application code, making it more complex and harder to maintain. Cross-cutting concerns in particular need to be replicated across multiple applications and are often copied and pasted from one code base to another.

In Kubernetes, we can avoid bundling cross-cutting concerns into the application code by running them in another container apart from the main application container. The adapter pattern transforms the output produced by the application to make it consumable in the format needed by another part of the system. Figure 4-4 illustrates a concrete example of the adapter pattern.

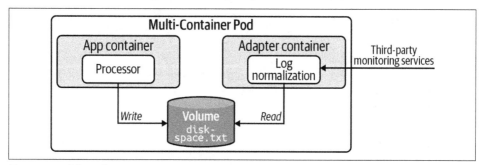

Figure 4-4. The adapter pattern in action

The business application running the main container produces timestamped information—in this case, the available disk space—and writes it to the file *diskspace.txt*. As part of the architecture, we want to consume the file from a third-party monitoring application. The problem is that the external application requires the information to exclude the timestamp. Now, we could change the logging format to avoid writing the timestamp, but what do we do if we actually want to know when the log entry has been written? This is where the adapter pattern can help. A sidecar container executes transformation logic that turns the log entries into the format needed by the external system without having to change application logic.

The YAML manifest shown in Example 4-3 illustrates what this implementation of the adapter pattern could look like. The `app` container produces a new log entry every five seconds. The `transformer` container consumes the contents of the file, removes the timestamp, and writes it to a new file. Both containers have access to the same mount path through a Volume.

Example 4-3. An exemplary adapter pattern implementation

```
apiVersion: v1
kind: Pod
metadata:
```

```
      name: adapter
spec:
  containers:
  - args:
    - /bin/sh
    - -c
    - 'while true; do echo "$(date) | $(du -sh ~)" >> /var/logs/diskspace.txt; \
        sleep 5; done;'
    image: busybox
    name: app
    volumeMounts:
      - name: config-volume
        mountPath: /var/logs
  - image: busybox
    name: transformer
    args:
    - /bin/sh
    - -c
    - 'sleep 20; while true; do while read LINE; do echo "$LINE" | cut -f2 -d"|" \
        >> $(date +%Y-%m-%d-%H-%M-%S)-transformed.txt; done < \
        /var/logs/diskspace.txt; sleep 20; done;'
    volumeMounts:
    - name: config-volume
      mountPath: /var/logs
  volumes:
  - name: config-volume
    emptyDir: {}
```

After creating the Pod, we'll find two running containers. We should be able to locate the original file, */var/logs/diskspace.txt*, after shelling into the transformer container. The transformed data exists in a separate file in the user home directory:

```
$ kubectl create -f adapter.yaml
pod/adapter created
$ kubectl get pods adapter
NAME       READY   STATUS    RESTARTS   AGE
adapter    2/2     Running   0          10s
$ kubectl exec adapter --container=transformer -it -- /bin/sh
/ # cat /var/logs/diskspace.txt
Sun Jul 19 20:28:07 UTC 2020 | 4.0K     /root
Sun Jul 19 20:28:12 UTC 2020 | 4.0K     /root
/ # ls -l
total 40
-rw-r--r-- 1  root  root  60 Jul 19 20:28 2020-07-19-20-28-28-transformed.txt
...
/ # cat 2020-07-19-20-28-28-transformed.txt
  4.0K    /root
  4.0K    /root
```

The Ambassador Pattern

Another important design pattern covered by the CKAD is the ambassador pattern. The ambassador pattern provides a proxy for communicating with external services.

There are many use cases that can justify the introduction of the ambassador pattern. The overarching goal is to hide and/or abstract the complexity of interacting with other parts of the system. Typical responsibilities include retry logic upon a request failure, security concerns like providing authentication or authorization, or monitoring latency or resource usage. Figure 4-5 shows the higher-level picture.

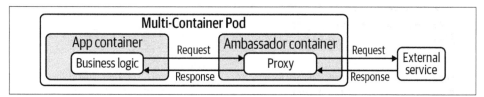

Figure 4-5. The ambassador pattern in action

In this example, we'll want to implement rate-limiting functionality for HTTP(S) calls to an external service. For example, the requirements for the rate limiter could say that an application can only make a maximum of 5 calls every 15 minutes. Instead of strongly coupling the rate-limiting logic to the application code, it will be provided by an ambassador container. Any calls made from the business application need to be funneled through the ambassador container. Example 4-4 shows a Node.js-based rate limiter implementation that makes calls to the external service Postman (*https://www.postman.com*).

Example 4-4. Node.js HTTP rate limiter implementation

```
const express = require('express');
const app = express();
const rateLimit = require('express-rate-limit');
const https = require('https');

const rateLimiter = rateLimit({
  windowMs: 15 * 60 * 1000,
  max: 5,
  message:
    'Too many requests have been made from this IP, please try again after an hour'
});

app.get('/test', rateLimiter, function (req, res) {
  console.log('Received request...');
  var id = req.query.id;
  var url = 'https://postman-echo.com/get?test=' + id;
  console.log("Calling URL %s", url);
```

```
  https.get(url, (resp) => {
    let data = '';

    resp.on('data', (chunk) => {
      data += chunk;
    });

    resp.on('end', () => {
      res.send(data);
    });

    }).on("error", (err) => {
      res.send(err.message);
    });
})

var server = app.listen(8081, function () {
  var port = server.address().port
  console.log("Ambassador listening on port %s...", port)
})
```

The corresponding Pod shown in Example 4-5 runs the main application container on a different port than the ambassador container. Every call to the HTTP endpoint of the container named business-app would delegate to the HTTP endpoint of the container named ambassador. It's important to mention that containers running inside of the same Pod can communicate via localhost. No additional networking configuration is required.

Example 4-5. An exemplary ambassador pattern implementation

```
apiVersion: v1
kind: Pod
metadata:
  name: rate-limiter
spec:
  containers:
  - name: business-app
    image: bmuschko/nodejs-business-app:1.0.0
    ports:
    - containerPort: 8080
  - name: ambassador
    image: bmuschko/nodejs-ambassador:1.0.0
    ports:
    - containerPort: 8081
```

Let's test the functionality. First, we'll create the Pod, shell into the container that runs the business application, and execute a series of curl commands. The first five calls will be allowed to the external service. On the sixth call, we'll receive an error message, as the rate limit has been reached within the given time frame:

```
$ kubectl create -f ambassador.yaml
pod/rate-limiter created
$ kubectl get pods rate-limiter
NAME            READY   STATUS    RESTARTS   AGE
rate-limiter    2/2     Running   0          5s
$ kubectl exec rate-limiter -it -c business-app -- /bin/sh
# curl localhost:8080/test
{"args":{"test":"123"},"headers":{"x-forwarded-proto":"https", \
"x-forwarded-port":"443","host":"postman-echo.com", \
"x-amzn-trace-id":"Root=1-5f177dba-e736991e882d12fcffd23f34"}, \
"url":"https://postman-echo.com/get?test=123"}
...
# curl localhost:8080/test
Too many requests have been made from this IP, please try again after an hour
```

Summary

Real-world scenarios call for running multiple containers inside of a Pod. An init container helps with setting the stage for the main application container by executing initializing logic. Once the initialized logic has been processed, the container will be terminated. The main application container only starts if the init container ran through its functionality successfully.

Kubernetes enables implementing software engineering best practices like separation of concerns and the single-responsibility principle. Cross-cutting concerns or helper functionality can be run in a so-called sidecar container. A sidecar container lives alongside the main application container within the same Pod and fulfills this exact role.

We talked about other design patterns that involve multiple containers per Pod: the adapter pattern and the ambassador pattern. The adapter pattern helps with "translating" data produced by the application so that it becomes consumable by third-party services. The ambassador pattern acts as a proxy for the application container when communicating with external services by abstracting the "how."

Exam Essentials

Understand the need for running multiple containers in a Pod
Pods can run multiple containers. You will need to understand the difference between init containers and sidecar containers and their respective lifecycles. Practice accessing a specific container in a multi-container Pod with the help of the command-line option `--container`.

Know how to create an init container

Init containers see a lot of use in enterprise Kubernetes cluster environments. Understand the need for using them in their respective scenarios. Practice defining a Pod with one or even more init containers and observe their linear execution when creating the Pod. It's important to experience the behavior of a Pod in failure situations that occur in an init container.

Understand sidecar patterns and how to implement them

Sidecar containers are best understood by implementing a scenario for one of the established patterns. Based on what you've learned, come up with your own applicable use case and create a multi-container Pod to solve it. It's helpful to be able to identify sidecar patterns and understand why they are important in practice and how to stand them up yourself. While implementing your own sidecars, you may notice that you have to brush up on your knowledge of bash.

Sample Exercises

Solutions to these exercises are available in the Appendix.

1. Create a YAML manifest for a Pod named `complex-pod`. The main application container named `app` should use the image `nginx` and expose the container port 80. Modify the YAML manifest so that the Pod defines an init container named `setup` that uses the image `busybox`. The init container runs the command `wget -O- google.com`.

2. Create the Pod from the YAML manifest.

3. Download the logs of the init container. You should see the output of the `wget` command.

4. Open an interactive shell to the main application container and run the `ls` command. Exit out of the container.

5. Force-delete the Pod.

6. Create a YAML manifest for a Pod named `data-exchange`. The main application container named `main-app` should use the image `busybox`. The container runs a command that writes a new file every 30 seconds in an infinite loop in the directory */var/app/data*. The filename follows the pattern *{counter++}-data.txt*. The variable counter is incremented every interval and starts with the value 1.

7. Modify the YAML manifest by adding a sidecar container named `sidecar`. The sidecar container uses the image `busybox` and runs a command that counts the number of files produced by the `main-app` container every 60 seconds in an infinite loop. The command writes the number of files to standard output.

8. Define a Volume of type `emptyDir`. Mount the path */var/app/data* for both containers.

9. Create the Pod. Tail the logs of the sidecar container.

10. Delete the Pod.

## CHAPTER 5

Observability

Applications running in containers do not operate under the premise of "fire and for-get." Once the container has been started, you'll want to know if the application is ready for consumption and is still working as expected in an hour, a week, or a month. The Observability section of the exam addresses the concern.

In this chapter, we'll discuss container health probes—more specifically, startup, read-iness, and liveness probes. You'll learn about the different health verification methods and how to define them for the proper use cases. Moreover, the exam expects you to be familiar with strategies for debugging a misconfigured or misbehaving Kubernetes object. We'll round out the chapter by ttalking about monitoring cluster nodes and Pods.

At a high level, this chapter covers the following concepts:

- Readiness probe
- Liveness probe
- Startup probe
- Troubleshooting Kubernetes objects
- Monitoring

Understanding Health Probing

Even with the best automated test coverage, it's nearly impossible to find all bugs before deploying software to a production environment. That's especially true for fail-ure situations that only occur after operating the software for an extended period of time. It's not uncommon to see memory leaks, deadlocks, infinite loops, and similar conditions crop up once the application has been put under load by end users.

Proper monitoring can help with identifying those issues; however, you still need to take an action to mitigate the situation. First of all, you'll likely want to restart the application to prevent further outages. Second, the development team needs to identify the underlying root cause and fix the application's code.

Kubernetes provides a concept called *health probing* to automate the detection and correction of such issues. You can configure a container to execute a periodic mini-process that checks for certain conditions. These processes are defined as follows:

Readiness probe
> Even after an application has been started up, it may still need to execute configuration procedures—for example, connecting to a database and preparing data. This probe checks if the application is ready to serve incoming requests. Figure 5-1 shows the readiness probe.

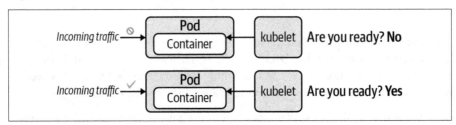

Figure 5-1. A readiness probe checks if the application is ready to accept traffic

Liveness probe
> Once the application is running, we'll want to make sure that it still works as expected without issues. This probe periodically checks for the application's responsiveness. Kubernetes restarts the Pod automatically if the probe considers the application be in an unhealthy state, as shown in Figure 5-2.

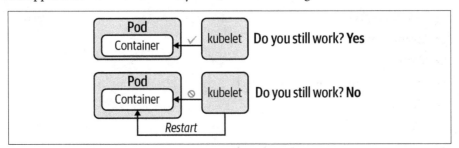

Figure 5-2. A liveness probe checks if the application is still considered healthy

Startup probe

Legacy applications in particular can take a long time to start up—we're talking minutes sometimes. This probe can be instantiated to wait for a predefined amount of time before a liveness probe is allowed to start probing. By setting up a startup probe, you can prevent overwhelming the application process with probing requests. Startup probes kill the container if the application couldn't start within the set time frame. Figure 5-3 illustrates the behavior of a startup probe.

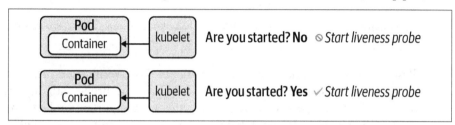

Figure 5-3. A startup probe checks if the application is started

Each probe offers three distinct methods to verify the health of a container. You can define one or many of the health verification methods for a container. Table 5-1 describes the available health verification methods, their corresponding YAML attribute, and their runtime behavior.

Table 5-1. Available health verification methods

Method	Option	Description
Custom command	`exec.command`	Executes a command inside of the container (e.g., a `cat` command) and checks its exit code. Kubernetes considers a zero exit code to be successful. A non-zero exit code indicates an error.
HTTP GET request	`httpGet`	Sends an HTTP GET request to an endpoint exposed by the application. An HTTP response code in the range of 200 and 399 indicates success. Any other response code is regarded as an error.
TCP socket connection	`tcpSocket`	Tries to open a TCP socket connection to a port. If the connection could be established, the probing attempt was successful. The inability to connect is accounted for as an error.

Every probe offers a set of attributes that can further configure the runtime behavior, as shown in Table 5-2. For more information, see the API of the Probe (*https:// oreil.ly/pk2b8*) object.

Table 5-2. Attributes for fine-tuning the health check runtime behavior

Attribute	Default value	Description
initialDelaySeconds	0	Delay in seconds until first check is executed.
periodSeconds	10	Interval for executing a check (e.g., every 20 seconds).
timeoutSeconds	1	Maximum number of seconds until check operation times out.
successThreshold	1	Number of successful check attempts until probe is considered successful after a failure.
failureThreshold	3	Number of failures for check attempts before probe is marked failed and takes action.

The following sections will demonstrate the usage of those verification methods for different probe types. Remember that you can combine any probe with any health check method. From an operational perspective, the most important probe to implement is the readiness probe. Without defining liveness and startup probes, the Kubernetes control plane components will handle the majority of the default behavior.

Readiness Probe

In this scenario, we'll want to define a readiness probe for a Node.js application. The Node.js application exposes an HTTP endpoint on the root context path and runs on port 3000. Dealing with a web-based application makes an HTTP GET request a perfect fit for probing its readiness. You can find the source code of the application in the book's GitHub repository (*https://oreil.ly/ZTj_Y*).

In the YAML manifest shown in Example 5-1, the readiness probe executes its first check after two seconds and repeats checking every eight seconds thereafter. All other attributes use the default values. A readiness probe will continue to periodically check, even after the application has been successfully started.

Example 5-1. A readiness probe that uses an HTTP GET request

```
apiVersion: v1
kind: Pod
metadata:
  name: readiness-pod
spec:
  containers:
  - image: bmuschko/nodejs-hello-world:1.0.0
    name: hello-world
    ports:
    - name: nodejs-port
      containerPort: 3000
    readinessProbe:
      httpGet:
```

```
    path: /
    port: nodejs-port
  initialDelaySeconds: 2
  periodSeconds: 8
```

Create a Pod by pointing the `create` command to the YAML manifest. During the Pod's startup process, it's very possible that the status shows `Running` but the container isn't ready to accept incoming requests yet, as indicated by 0/1 under the READY column:

```
$ kubectl create -f readiness-probe.yaml
pod/readiness-pod created
$ kubectl get pod readiness-pod
NAME                READY   STATUS    RESTARTS   AGE
pod/readiness-pod   0/1     Running   0          6s
$ kubectl get pod readiness-pod
NAME                READY   STATUS    RESTARTS   AGE
pod/readiness-pod   1/1     Running   0          68s
$ kubectl describe pod readiness-pod
...
Containers:
  hello-world:
    ...
    Readiness:        http-get http://:nodejs-port/ delay=2s timeout=1s \
                      period=8s #success=1 #failure=3
...
```

Liveness Probe

A liveness probe checks if the application is still working as expected down the road. For the purpose of demonstrating a liveness probe, we'll use a custom command. A custom command is probably the most flexible way to verify the health of a container, as it allows for calling any command available to the container. That can either be a command-line tool that comes with the base image or a tool that you install as part of the containization process.

In Example 5-2, we'll have the application create and update a file, */tmp/heartbeat.txt*, to show that it's still alive. We'll do this by it run the Unix `touch` command every five seconds. The probe will periodically check if the modification timestamp of the file is older than one minute. If it is, then Kubernetes can assume that the application isn't functioning as expected and will restart the container.

Example 5-2. A liveness probe that uses a custom command

```
apiVersion: v1
kind: Pod
metadata:
  name: liveness-pod
```

```
spec:
  containers:
  - image: busybox
    name: app
    args:
    - /bin/sh
    - -c
    - 'while true; do touch /tmp/heartbeat.txt; sleep 5; done;'
    livenessProbe:
      exec:
        command:
        - test `find /tmp/heartbeat.txt -mmin -1`
      initialDelaySeconds: 5
      periodSeconds: 30
```

The following command uses the YAML manifest shown in Example 5-2 stored in the file *liveness-probe.yaml* to create the Pod. Describing the Pod renders information on the liveness probe. Not only can we inspect the custom command and its configuration, we can also see how many times the container has been restarted upon a probing failure:

```
$ kubectl create -f liveness-probe.yaml
pod/liveness-pod created
$ kubectl get pod liveness-pod
NAME                   READY   STATUS    RESTARTS   AGE
pod/liveness-pod       1/1     Running   0          22s
$ kubectl describe pod liveness-pod
...
Containers:
  app:
    ...
    Restart Count:  0
    Liveness:       exec [test `find /tmp/heartbeat.txt -mmin -1`] delay=5s \
                    timeout=1s period=30s #success=1 #failure=3
...
```

Startup Probe

The purpose of a startup probe is to figure out when an application is fully started. Defining the probe is especially useful for an application that takes a long time to start up. The kubelet puts the readiness and liveness probes on hold while the startup probe is running. A startup probe finishes its operation under one of the following conditions:

1. If it could verify that the application has been started.

2. If the application doesn't respond within the timeout period.

To demonstrate the functionality of the startup probe, Example 5-3 defines a Pod that runs the Apache HTTP server (*https://oreil.ly/Hzfxq*) in a container. By default, the image exposes the container port 80, and that's what we're probing for using a TCP socket connection.

Example 5-3. A startup probe that uses a TCP socket connection

```
apiVersion: v1
kind: Pod
metadata:
  name: startup-pod
spec:
  containers:
  - image: httpd:2.4.46
    name: http-server
    startupProbe:
      tcpSocket:
        port: 80
      initialDelaySeconds: 3
      periodSeconds: 15
```

As you can see in the following terminal output, the describe command can retrieve the configuration of a startup probe as well:

```
$ kubectl create -f startup-probe.yaml
pod/startup-pod created
$ kubectl get pod startup-pod
NAME                READY    STATUS     RESTARTS    AGE
pod/startup-pod     1/1      Running    0           31s
$ kubectl describe pod startup-pod
...
Containers:
  http-server:
      ...
    Startup:         tcp-socket :80 delay=3s timeout=1s period=15s \
                     #success=1 #failure=3
...
```

Debugging in Kubernetes

When operating an application in a production Kubernetes cluster, it's almost inevitable that you'll come across failure situations. You can't completely leave this job up to the Kubernetes adminstrator—it's your responsibility as an application developer to be able to troubleshoot issues for the Kubernetes objects you designed and deployed.

In this section, we're going to have a look at debugging strategies that can help with identifying the root cause of an issue so that you can take action and correct the failure appropriately. The strategies discussed here start with the high-level perspective of a Kubernetes object and then drill into more detail as needed.

Troubleshooting Pods

In most cases, creating a Pod is no issue. You simply emit the run, `create`, or `apply` commands to instantiate the Pod. If the YAML manifest is formed properly, Kubernetes accepts your request, so the assumption is that everything works as expected. To verify the correct behavior, the first thing you'll want to do is to check the high-level runtime information of the Pod. The operation could involve other Kubernetes objects like a Deployment responsible for rolling out multiple replicas of a Pod.

Debugging YAML manifests

If you're somewhat new to Kubernetes, you may run into trouble when crafting properly formed YAML manifests. Any incorrect indentation, spelling issue, attribute name, or enumeration will cause a problem during object creation. During the CKAD exam, you won't have any tools available to verify the correctness of a YAML manifest. While practicing, you might find the browser-based application Kube YAML (*https://kubeyaml.com*) helpful. You can simply copy and paste the YAML manifest as text and receive feedback about its correctness. Figure 5-4 illustrates the behavior of the application for a YAML manifest that uses an incorrect attribute name.

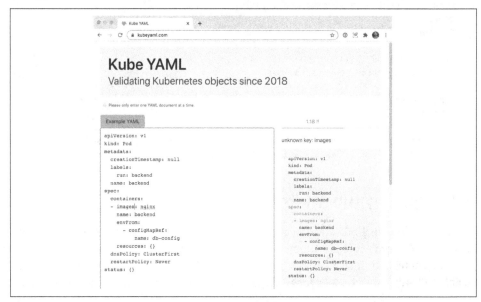

Figure 5-4. YAML manifest validation with Kube YAML

Retrieving high-level information

To retrieve the information, run either the `kubectl get pods` command for just the Pods running in the namespace or the `kubectl get all` command to retrieve the most prominent object types in the namespace (which includes Deployments). You will want to have a look at the columns READY, STATUS, and RESTARTS. In the optimal case, the number of ready containers matches the number of containers expected to be created by the Pod. For a single-container Pod, the READY column would say 1/1. The status should say Running to indicate that the Pod entered the proper lifecycle state. Be aware that it's totally possible that a Pod renders a Running state, but the application isn't actually working properly. If the number of restarts is greater than 0, then you might want to check the logic of the liveness probe (if defined) and identify the reason why a restart was necessary.

The following Pod observes the status ErrImagePull and makes 0/1 containers available to incoming traffic. In short, this Pod has a problem:

```
$ kubectl get pods
NAME                  READY   STATUS         RESTARTS   AGE
pod/misbehaving-pod   0/1     ErrImagePull   0          2s
```

After working with Kubernetes for a while, you'll automatically recognize common error conditions. Table 5-3 lists some of those error statuses and explains how to fix them.

Table 5-3. Common Pod error statuses

Status	Root cause	Potential fix
`ImagePullBackOff` or `ErrImagePull`	Image could not be pulled from registry.	Check correct image name, check that image name exists in registry, verify network access from node to registry, ensure proper authentication.
`CrashLoopBackOff`	Application or command run in container crashes.	Check command executed in container, ensure that image can properly execute (e.g., by creating a container with Docker).
`CreateContainerConfigError`	ConfigMap or Secret referenced by container cannot be found.	Check correct name of the configuration object, verify the existence of the configuration object in the namespace.

Inspecting events

It's totally possible that you'll not encounter any of those error statuses. But there's still a chance of the Pod having a configuration issue. You can retrieve detailed information about the Pod and its events using the `kubectl describe pod` command to inspect its events. The following output belongs to a Pod that tries to mount a Secret that doesn't exist. Instead of rendering a specific error message, the Pod gets stuck with the status `ContainerCreating`:

```
$ kubectl get pods
NAME            READY    STATUS               RESTARTS    AGE
secret-pod      0/1      ContainerCreating    0           4m57s
$ kubectl describe pod secret-pod
...
Events:
Type     Reason       Age                     From          Message
----     ------       ----                    ----          -------
Normal   Scheduled    <unknown>               default-scheduler Successfully assigned \
                                                            default/secret-pod to \
                                                            minikube
Warning  FailedMount  3m15s                   kubelet, minikube Unable to attach or \
                                                            mount volumes: \
                                                            unmounted \
                                                            volumes=[mysecret], \
                                                            unattached volumes= \
                                                            [default-token-bf8rh \
                                                            mysecret]: timed out \
                                                            waiting for the \
                                                            condition
Warning  FailedMount  68s (x10 over 5m18s) kubelet, minikube MountVolume.SetUp \
                                                            failed for volume \
                                                            "mysecret" : secret \
                                                            "mysecret" not found
Warning  FailedMount  61s                     kubelet, minikube Unable to attach or \
                                                            mount volumes: \
                                                            unmounted volumes= \
                                                            [mysecret], unattached \
                                                            volumes=[mysecret \
                                                            default-token-bf8rh]: \
                                                            timed out waiting for \
                                                            the condition
```

Another helpful command is kubectl get events. The output of the command lists the events across all Pods for a given namespace. You can use additional command-line options to further filter and sort events:

```
$ kubectl get events
LAST SEEN   TYPE      REASON            OBJECT               MESSAGE
3m14s       Warning   BackOff           pod/custom-cmd       Back-off restarting \
                                                             failed container
2s          Warning   FailedNeedsStart  cronjob/google-ping  Cannot determine if \
                                                             job needs to be \
                                                             started: too many \
                                                             missed start time \
                                                             (> 100). Set or \
                                                             decrease .spec. \
                                                             startingDeadline \
                                                             Seconds or check \
                                                             clock skew
```

Inspecting logs

When debugging a Pod, the next level of details can be retrieved by downloading and inspecting its logs. You may or may not find additional information that points to the root cause of a misbehaving Pod. It's definitely worth a look. The YAML manifest shown in Example 5-4 defines a Pod running a shell command.

Example 5-4. A Pod running a failing shell command

```
apiVersion: v1
kind: Pod
metadata:
  name: incorrect-cmd-pod
spec:
  containers:
  - name: test-container
    image: busybox
    command: ["/bin/sh", "-c", "unknown"]
```

After creating the object, the Pod fails with the status `CrashLoopBackOff`. Running the `logs` command reveals that the command run in the container has an issue:

```
$ kubectl create -f crash-loop-backoff.yaml
pod/incorrect-cmd-pod created
$ kubectl get pods incorrect-cmd-pod
NAME                READY    STATUS            RESTARTS    AGE
incorrect-cmd-pod   0/1      CrashLoopBackOff  5           3m20s
$ kubectl logs incorrect-cmd-pod
/bin/sh: unknown: not found
```

The `logs` command provides two helpful options I'd like to mention here. The option `-f` streams the logs, meaning you'll see new log entries as they're being produced in real time. The option `--previous` gets the logs from the previous instantiation of a container, which is helpful if the container has been restarted.

Opening an Interactive Shell

If any of the previous commands don't point you to the root cause of the failing Pod, it's time to open an interactive shell to a container. As an application developer, you'll probably know best what behavior to expect from the application at runtime. Ensure that the correct configuration has been created and inspect the running processes by using the Unix or Windows utility tools, depending on the image run in the container.

Say you encounter a situation where a Pod seems to work properly on the surface, as shown in Example 5-5.

Example 5-5. A Pod periodically writing the current date to a file

```
apiVersion: v1
kind: Pod
metadata:
  name: failing-pod
spec:
  containers:
  - args:
    - /bin/sh
    - -c
    - while true; do echo $(date) >> ~/tmp/curr-date.txt; sleep \
      5; done;
    image: busybox
    name: failing-pod
```

After creating the Pod, you check the status. It says Running; however, when making a request to the application, the endpoint reports an error. Next, you check the logs. The log output renders an error message that points to a nonexistent directory. Apparently, the directory hasn't been set up correctly but is needed by the application:

```
$ kubectl create -f failing-pod.yaml
pod/failing-pod created
$ kubectl get pods failing-pod
NAME          READY   STATUS    RESTARTS   AGE
failing-pod   1/1     Running   0          5s
$ kubectl logs failing-pod
/bin/sh: can't create /root/tmp/curr-date.txt: nonexistent directory
```

The exec command opens an interactive shell to further investigate the issue. Below, we're using the Unix tools mkdir, cd, and ls inside of the running container to fix the problem. Obviously, the better mitigation strategy is to create the directory from the application or provide an instruction in the Dockerfile:

```
$ kubectl exec failing-pod -it -- /bin/sh
# mkdir -p ~/tmp
# cd ~/tmp
# ls -l
total 4
-rw-r--r-- 1 root root 112 May 9 23:52 curr-date.txt
```

Using an Ephemeral Container

Some images run in a container are designed to be very minimalistic. For example, the Google distroless (*https://oreil.ly/EHfQZ*) images don't have any Unix utility tools preinstalled. You can't even open a shell to a container, as it doesn't even come with a shell. That's the case for the image k8s.gcr.io/pause:3.1, a minimal, distroless image that keeps the container running, used in Example 5-6.

Example 5-6. Running a distroless image

```
apiVersion: v1
kind: Pod
metadata:
  name: minimal-pod
spec:
  containers:
  - image: k8s.gcr.io/pause:3.1
    name: pause
```

As you can see in the following exec command, the image doesn't provide a shell:

```
$ kubectl create -f minimal-pod.yaml
pod/minimal-pod created
$ kubectl get pods minimal-pod
NAME          READY    STATUS     RESTARTS    AGE
minimal-pod   1/1      Running    0           8s
$ kubectl exec minimal-pod -it -- /bin/sh
OCI runtime exec failed: exec failed: container_linux.go:349: starting \
container process caused "exec: \"/bin/sh\": stat /bin/sh: no such file \
or directory": unknown
command terminated with exit code 126
```

Kubernetes offers the concept of ephemeral containers (*https://oreil.ly/4OfB1*). Those containers are meant to be disposable and can be deployed for troubleshooting minimal containers that would usually not allow the usage of the exec command.

> Ephemeral containers are still considered an experimental feature. You will have to explicitly enable the feature with the feature flag `--feature-gates` when starting up the Kubernetes cluster. For example, starting Minikube with this feature can be achieved by using the command `minikube start --feature-gates=EphemeralContainers=true`.

Kubernetes 1.18 introduced a new debug command that can add an ephemeral container to a running Pod for debugging purposes. The following command adds the ephemeral container running the image busybox to the Pod named minimal-pod and opens an interactive shell for it:

```
$ kubectl alpha debug -it minimal-pod --image=busybox
Defaulting debug container name to debugger-jf98g.
If you don't see a command prompt, try pressing enter.
/ # pwd
/
/ # exit
Session ended, resume using 'kubectl alpha attach minimal-pod -c \
debugger-jf98g -i -t' command when the pod is running
```

Troubleshooting Services

A Service provides a unified network interface for Pods. For full coverage on networking aspects in Kubernetes, see Chapter 7, *Services & Networking*. Here, I want to point out troubleshooting techniques for this primitive.

In case you can't reach the Pods that should map to the Service, start by ensuring that the label selector matches with the assigned labels of the Pods. You can query the information by describing the Service and then render the labels of the available Pods with the option `--show-labels`. The following example does not have matching labels and therefore wouldn't apply to any of the Pods running in the namespace:

```
$ kubectl describe service myservice
...
Selector:          app=myapp
...
$ kubectl get pods --show-labels
NAME                        READY   STATUS    RESTARTS   AGE      LABELS
myapp-68bf896d89-qfhlv      1/1     Running   0          7m39s    app=hello
myapp-68bf896d89-tzt55      1/1     Running   0          7m37s    app=world
```

Alternatively, you can also query the endpoints of the Service instance. Say you expected three Pods to be selected by a matching label but only two have been exposed by the Service. You'll want to look at the label selection criteria:

```
$ kubectl get endpoints myservice
NAME         ENDPOINTS                        AGE
myservice    172.17.0.5:80,172.17.0.6:80      9m31s
```

A common source of confusion is the type of a Service. By default, the Service type is `ClusterIP`, which means that a Pod can only be reached through the Service if queried from the same node inside of the cluster. First, check the Service type. If you think that `ClusterIP` is the proper type you wanted to assign, open an interactive shell from a temporary Pod inside the cluster and run a `curl` or `wget` command:

```
$ kubectl get services
NAME         TYPE        CLUSTER-IP       EXTERNAL-IP   PORT(S)   AGE
myservice    ClusterIP   10.99.155.165    <none>        80/TCP    15m
$ kubectl run tmp --image=busybox -it --rm -- wget -O- 10.99.155.165:80
....
```

Finally, check if the port mapping from the target port of the Service to the container port of the Pod is configured correctly. Both ports need to match:

```
$ kubectl get service myapp -o yaml | grep targetPort:
    targetPort: 80
$ kubectl get pods myapp-68bf896d89-qfhlv -o yaml | grep containerPort:
    - containerPort: 80
```

Monitoring

Deploying software to a Kubernetes cluster is only the start of operating an application long-term. Developers need to understand resource consumption patterns and behaviors of their applications with the goal of providing a scalable and reliable service.

In the Kubernetes world, monitoring tools like Prometheus and Datadog help with collecting, processing, and visualizing the information over time. The CKAD exam does not expect you to be familiar with commercial monitoring, logging, tracing, and aggregation tools; however, it is helpful to gain a rough understanding of the underlying Kubernetes infrastructure responsible for collecting usage metrics, such as a container's CPU and memory usage.

This responsibility falls into the hands of the metrics server (*https://oreil.ly/lLTTh*), a cluster-wide aggregator of resource usage data. Refer to the documentation for more information on its installation process. If you're using Minikube as your practice environment, enabling the metrics-server add-on (*https://oreil.ly/qRVcR*) is straightforward using the following command:

```
$ minikube addons enable metrics-server
The 'metrics-server' addon is enabled
```

You can now query for metrics of cluster nodes and Pods with the top command:

```
$ kubectl top nodes
NAME       CPU(cores)   CPU%   MEMORY(bytes)   MEMORY%
minikube   283m         14%    1262Mi          32%
$ kubectl top pod frontend
NAME       CPU(cores)   MEMORY(bytes)
frontend   0m           2Mi
```

Summary

Diagnosing the root cause of runtime issues for an application operated in a Kubernetes cluster can be difficult and tedious. Observability covers health probing, logging, monitoring, and debugging of cloud native services.

One of the important takeaways is the fact that Kubernetes can take action upon certain failure conditions automatically without the need for manual intervention from a system administrator or application developer. In this chapter, we looked at all available health probe types you can define for a Pod. A health probe is a periodically running mini-process that asks the application running in a container for its status. You can think of it as feeling the pulse of your system.

The readiness probe ensures that incoming traffic is only accepted by the container if the application runs properly. The liveness probe makes sure that the application is functioning as expected and will restart the container if necessary. The startup probe pauses readiness and liveness probes until application startup has been completed. In practice, you'll often find that a container defines all three probes.

We also discussed strategies for approaching failed or misbehaving Pods. The main goal is to diagnose the root cause of a failure and then fix it by taking the right action. Troubleshooting Pods doesn't have to be hard. With the right `kubectl` commands in your tool belt, you can rule out root causes one by one to get a clearer picture.

The Kubernetes ecosystem provides a lot of options for collecting and processing metrics of your cluster over time. Among those options are commercial monitoring tools like Prometheus and Datadog. Many of those tools use the metrics server as the source of truth for those metrics. We briefly touched on the installation process and the `kubectl top` command for retrieving metrics from the command line.

Exam Essentials

Understand all health probes
In preparation for the exam, put the majority of effort in this section into understanding and using health probes. You should understand the purpose of startup, readiness, and liveness probes and practice how to configure them. In your Kubernetes cluster, try to emulate success and failure conditions to see the effects of a probe and the actions they take.

Know how to debug Kubernetes objects
In this chapter, we mainly focused on troubleshooting problematic Pods and Services. Practice all relevant `kubectl` commands that can help with diagnosing issues. Refer to the Kubernetes documentation (*https://oreil.ly/mBFDX*) to learn more about debugging other Kubernetes resource types.

Have a basic understanding of monitoring
Monitoring a Kubernetes cluster is an important aspect of successfully operating in a real-world environment. This topic mostly consists of reading up on commercial monitoring products and the metrics that can be gathered.

Sample Exercises

Solutions to these exercises are available in the Appendix.

1. Define a new Pod named `web-server` with the image `nginx` in a YAML manifest. Expose the container port 80. Do not create the Pod yet.

2. For the container, declare a startup probe of type `httpGet`. Verify that the root context endpoint can be called. Use the default configuration for the probe.

3. For the container, declare a readiness probe of type httpGet. Verify that the root context endpoint can be called. Wait five seconds before checking for the first time.

4. For the container, declare a liveness probe of type httpGet. Verify that the root context endpoint can be called. Wait 10 seconds before checking for the first time. The probe should run the check every 30 seconds.

5. Create the Pod and follow the lifecycle phases of the Pod during the process.

6. Inspect the runtime details of the probes of the Pod.

7. Retrieve the metrics of the Pod (e.g., CPU and memory) from the metrics server.

8. Create a Pod named custom-cmd with the image busybox. The container should run the command top-analyzer with the command-line flag --all.

9. Inspect the status. How would you further troubleshoot the Pod to identify the root cause of the failure?

## CHAPTER 6

Pod Design

Of all the sections included in the CKAD curriculum, "Pod Design" has the most weight. This chapter is packed with a lot of concepts and intricacies you'll have to understand to increase your chances of passing the exam.

We'll start by reviewing labels, label selection, and annotations. As part of the discussion, we'll compare the commonalities and differences between labels and annotations. Labels are an essential tool for querying, filtering, and sorting Kubernetes objects. Annotations only represent descriptive metadata for Kubernetes objects but have no ability to be used for queries. You will learn how to assign and use both concepts.

A big selling point of Kubernetes is rooted in its scalability and replication features. To support those features, Kubernetes offers the Deployment primitive. We'll look at the creation of a Deployment scaled to multiple replicas, how to roll out a revision of your application, how to roll back to a previous revision, and how to use autoscalers to handle scaling concerns automatically based on the current workload.

Lastly, we'll touch on the Kubernetes primitives Job and CronJob. A Job models a one-time process—for example, a batch operation. The Pod and its encompassed containers stop running after the work has been completed. CronJobs run periodically according to their defined schedules. A good application for a CronJob is a task that needs to occur continuously (for example, a process that exports data). You will learn how to configure, run, and inspect a Job and a CronJob.

At a high level, this chapter covers the following concepts:

- Label
- Annotation
- Deployment

- ReplicaSet
- Horizontal Pod Autoscaler
- Job
- CronJob

Understanding Labels

Kubernetes lets you assign key-value pairs to objects so that you can use them later within a search query. Those key-value pairs are called *labels*. To draw an analogy, you can think of labels as tags for a blog post. A label describes a Kubernetes object in distinct terms (e.g., a category like "frontend" or "backend") but is not meant for elaborate, multi-word descriptions of its functionality. As part of the specification, Kubernetes limits the length of a label to a maximum of 63 characters and a range of allowed alphanumeric and separator characters.

Figure 6-1 shows the Pods named frontend, backend, and database. Each of the Pods declares a unique set of labels.

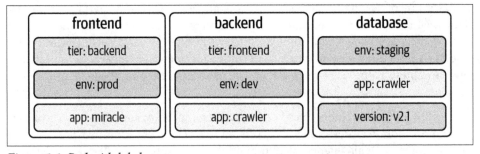

Figure 6-1. Pod with labels

It's common practice to assign one or many labels to an object at creation time; however, you can modify them as needed for a live object. When confronted with labels for the first time, they might seem like an insignificant feature—but their importance cannot be overstated. They're essential for understanding the runtime behavior of more advanced Kubernetes objects like a Deployment and a Service. Later in this chapter, we'll see the significance of labels in practice when talking about Deployments in more detail.

Declaring Labels

Labels can be declared imperatively with the run command or declaratively in the metadata.labels section in the YAML manifest. The command-line option --labels (or -l in its short form) defines a comma-separated list of labels when creating a Pod. The following command creates a new Pod with two labels from the command line:

```
$ kubectl run labeled-pod --image=nginx \
  --restart=Never --labels=tier=backend,env=dev
pod/labeled-pod created
```

Assigning labels to Kubernetes objects by editing the manifest requires a change to the `metadata` section. Example 6-1 shows the same Pod definition from the previous command if we were to start with the YAML manifest.

Example 6-1. A Pod defining two labels

```
apiVersion: v1
kind: Pod
metadata:
  name: labeled-pod
  labels:
    env: dev
    tier: backend
spec:
  containers:
  - image: nginx
    name: nginx
```

Inspecting Labels

You can inspect the labels assigned to a Kubernetes object from different angles. Here, we'll want to look at the most common ways to identify the labels of a Pod. As with any other runtime information, you can use the `describe` or `get` commands to retrieve the labels:

```
$ kubectl describe pod labeled-pod | grep -C 2 Labels:
...
Labels:        env=dev
               tier=backend
...
$ kubectl get pod labeled-pod -o yaml | grep -C 1 labels:
metadata:
  labels:
    env: dev
    tier: backend
...
```

If you want to list the labels for all object types or a specific object type, use the `--show-labels` command-line option. This option is convenient if you need to sift through a longer list of objects. The output automatically adds a new column named LABELS:

```
$ kubectl get pods --show-labels
NAME          READY  STATUS   RESTARTS  AGE   LABELS
labeled-pod   1/1    Running  0         38m   env=dev,tier=backend
```

Modifying Labels for a Live Object

At any given point in time, you can add or remove a label from an existing Kubernetes object, or simply modify an existing label. One way to achieve this is by editing the live object and changing the label definition in the `metadata.labels` section. The other option that offers a slightly faster turnaround is the `label` command. The following commands add a new label, change the value of the label, and then remove the label with the minus character:

```
$ kubectl label pod labeled-pod region=eu
pod/labeled-pod labeled
$ kubectl get pod labeled-pod --show-labels
NAME          READY  STATUS   RESTARTS  AGE   LABELS
labeled-pod   1/1    Running  0         22h   env=dev,region=eu,tier=backend
$ kubectl label pod labeled-pod region=us --overwrite
pod/labeled-pod labeled
$ kubectl get pod labeled-pod --show-labels
NAME          READY  STATUS   RESTARTS  AGE   LABELS
labeled-pod   1/1    Running  0         22h   env=dev,region=us,tier=backend
$ kubectl label pod labeled-pod region-
pod/labeled-pod labeled
$ kubectl get pod labeled-pod --show-labels
NAME          READY  STATUS   RESTARTS  AGE   LABELS
labeled-pod   1/1    Running  0         22h   env=dev,tier=backend
```

Using Label Selectors

Labels only really become meaningful when combined with the selection feature. A label selector uses a set of criteria to query for Kubernetes objects. For example, you could use a label selector to express "select all Pods with the label assignment env=dev, tier=frontend, and have a label with the key version independent of the assigned value," as shown in Figure 6-2.

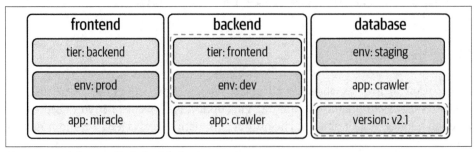

Figure 6-2. Selecting Pods by label criteria

Kubernetes offers two ways to select objects by labels: from the command line and within a manifest. Let's talk about both options.

Label Selection from the Command Line

On the command line, you can select objects by label using the --selector option, or -l in its short-form notation. Objects can be filtered by an equality-based requirement or a set-based requirement. Both requirement types can be combined in a single query.

An *equality-based requirement* can use the operators =, ==, or !=. You can separate multiple filter terms with a comma and then combine them with a boolean AND. At this time, equality-based label selection cannot express a boolean OR operation. A typical expression could say, "select all Pods with the label assignment env=prod."

A *set-based requirement* can filter objects based on a set of values using the operators in, notin, and exists. The in and notin operators work based on a boolean OR. A typical expression could say, "select all Pods with the label key env and the value prod or dev."

To demonstrate the functionality, we'll start by setting up three different Pods with labels. All kubectl commands use the command-line option --show-labels to compare the results with our expectations. The --show-labels option is not needed for label selection, though:

```
$ kubectl run frontend --image=nginx --restart=Never \
  --labels=env=prod,team=shiny
pod/frontend created
$ kubectl run backend --image=nginx --restart=Never \
  --labels=env=prod,team=legacy,app=v1.2.4
pod/backend created
$ kubectl run database --image=nginx --restart=Never \
  --labels=env=prod,team=storage
pod/database created
$ kubectl get pods --show-labels
NAME       READY   STATUS    RESTARTS   AGE   LABELS
backend    1/1     Running   0          37s   app=v1.2.4,env=prod,team=legacy
database   1/1     Running   0          32s   env=prod,team=storage
frontend   1/1     Running   0          42s   env=prod,team=shiny
```

We'll start by filtering the Pods with an equality-based requirement. Here, we are looking for all Pods with the label assignment env=prod. The result returns all three Pods:

```
$ kubectl get pods -l env=prod --show-labels
NAME       READY   STATUS    RESTARTS   AGE   LABELS
backend    1/1     Running   0          37s   app=v1.2.4,env=prod,team=legacy
database   1/1     Running   0          32s   env=prod,team=storage
frontend   1/1     Running   0          42s   env=prod,team=shiny
```

The next filter operation uses a set-based requirement. We are asking for all Pods that have the label key `team` with the values `storage` or `shiny`. The result only returns the Pods named `backend` and `frontend`:

```
$ kubectl get pods -l 'team in (shiny, legacy)' --show-labels
NAME       READY   STATUS    RESTARTS   AGE   LABELS
backend    1/1     Running   0          19m   app=v1.2.4,env=prod,team=legacy
frontend   1/1     Running   0          20m   env=prod,team=shiny
```

Finally, we'll combine an equality-based requirement with a set-based requirement. The result returns only the backend Pod:

```
$ kubectl get pods -l 'team in (shiny, legacy)',app=v1.2.4 --show-labels
NAME       READY   STATUS    RESTARTS   AGE   LABELS
backend    1/1     Running   0          29m   app=v1.2.4,env=prod,team=legacy
```

Label Selection in a Manifest

Some advanced Kubernetes objects such as Deployments, Services, or network policies act as configuration proxies for Pods. They usually select a set of Pods by labels and then provide added value. For example, a network policy controls network traffic from and to a set of Pods. Only the Pods with matching labels will apply the network rules. The following YAML manifest applies the network policy to Pods with the equality-based requirement `tier=frontend` (for more details on network policies, see Chapter 7, *Services & Networking*):

```
apiVersion: networking.k8s.io/v1
kind: NetworkPolicy
metadata:
  name: frontend-network-policy
spec:
  podSelector:
    matchLabels:
      tier: frontend
...
```

The way you define label selection in a manifest is based on the API version of the Kubernetes resources and may differ between different types. The content that follows in this and later chapters will make heavy use of label selection.

Understanding Annotations

Annotations are declared similarly to labels, but they serve a different purpose. They represent key-value pairs for providing descriptive metadata. The most important differentiator is that annotations cannot be used for querying or selecting objects. Typical examples of annotations may include SCM commit hash IDs, release information, or contact details for teams operating the object. Make sure to put the value of an annotation into single- or double-quotes if it contains special characters or spaces. Figure 6-3 illustrates a Pod with three annotations.

Figure 6-3. Pod with annotations

Declaring Annotations

The `kubectl run` command does not provide a command-line option for defining annotations that's similar to the one for labels. You will have to start by writing a YAML manifest and adding the desired annotations under `metadata.annotation`, as shown in Example 6-2.

Example 6-2. A Pod defining three annotations

```
apiVersion: v1
kind: Pod
metadata:
  name: annotated-pod
  annotations:
    commit: 866a8dc
    author: 'Benjamin Muschko'
    branch: 'bm/bugfix'
spec:
  containers:
  - image: nginx
    name: nginx
```

Inspecting Annotations

Similar to labels, you can use the `describe` or `get` commands to retrieve the assigned annotations:

```
$ kubectl describe pod annotated-pod | grep -C 2 Annotations:
...
Annotations:   author: Benjamin Muschko
               branch: bm/bugfix
               commit: 866a8dc
...
```

```
$ kubectl get pod annotated-pod -o yaml | grep -C 3 annotations:
metadata:
  annotations:
    author: Benjamin Muschko
    branch: bm/bugfix
    commit: 866a8dc
...
```

Modifying Annotations for a Live Object

The `annotate` command is the counterpart of the `labels` command but for annotations. As you can see in the following examples, the usage pattern is the same:

```
$ kubectl annotate pod annotated-pod oncall='800-555-1212'
pod/annotated-pod annotated
$ kubectl annotate pod annotated-pod oncall='800-555-2000' --overwrite
pod/annotated-pod annotated
$ kubectl annotate pod annotated-pod oncall-
pod/annotated-pod annotated
```

Understanding Deployments

At the beginning of this chapter, we discussed labels and label selection from all angles. We did so for a good reason. A Deployment is one of the Kubernetes primitives that uses labels as a foundational concept. If you didn't have a chance to fully brush up on labels, I'd urge you to review the content.

Running an application inside of a Pod is powerful, but scalability and reliability can become a problem. Say the load on your application increases during peak times or because of a growing user base, and you still have only one Pod instance that can serve up the application's functionality. With increased traffic comes higher resource consumption. Depending on the resource requirements of the container, the application may come to a grinding halt.

That's where a Deployment comes in. Within a Deployment, you can specify the number of Pods running your application with the exact same setup. Need to scale up? Simply bump up the number of replicas, and Kubernetes will take care of creating the Pods. Furthermore, the Deployment ensures that failing Pods are restarted so that the actual state matches with the desired state. Under the hood, a Deployment uses the Kubernetes primitive ReplicaSet, as shown in Figure 6-4.

The ReplicaSet's sole purpose is to *replicate* a guaranteed number of Pods with the same configuration. While the CKAD curriculum doesn't require explicit knowledge of a ReplicaSet, it's interesting to understand that the Deployment is the higher-level concept that manages the ReplicaSet internally with no involvement required by the end user.

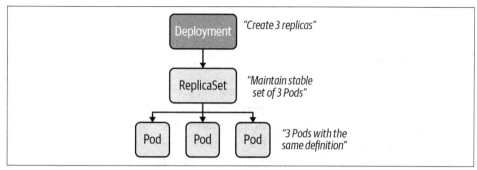

Figure 6-4. Replication of Pods with a Deployment

Creating Deployments

Deployments can be created imperatively with the `create deployment` command. The options you can provide to configure the Deployment are somewhat limited and do not resemble the ones you know from the `run` command. The following command creates a new Deployment that uses the image `nginx:1.14.2` for a single replica:

```
$ kubectl create deployment my-deploy --image=nginx:1.14.2
deployment.apps/my-deploy created
```

Often, you will find yourself generating and further modifying the YAML manifest. The following manifest creates a Deployment with a single replica. If you look closely, you will see label selection in action. The selector `spec.selector.matchLabels` matches on the key-value pair `app=my-deploy` with the label defined under the `template` section, as shown in Example 6-3.

Example 6-3. A YAML manifest defining a Deployment

```
apiVersion: apps/v1
kind: Deployment
metadata:
  name: my-deploy
  labels:
    app: my-deploy
spec:
  replicas: 1
  selector:
    matchLabels:
      app: my-deploy
  template:
    metadata:
      labels:
        app: my-deploy
    spec:
      containers:
```

```
    - name: nginx
      image: nginx:1.14.2
```

Listing Deployments

Once created, a Deployment and all of its corresponding objects can be listed. The
following `get` command lists all Deployments, Pods, and ReplicaSets. If a Pod or
ReplicaSet is managed by a Deployment, the name of the object will reflect that connection. For the Deployment named `my-deploy`, you will find at least one Pod and
one ReplicaSet with the prefix `my-deploy-` plus a random hash:

```
$ kubectl get deployments,pods,replicasets
NAME                         READY   UP-TO-DATE   AVAILABLE   AGE
deployment.apps/my-deploy    1/1     1            1           7m56s

NAME                             READY   STATUS    RESTARTS   AGE
pod/my-deploy-8448c488b5-mzx5g   1/1     Running   0          7m56s

NAME                                       DESIRED   CURRENT   READY   AGE
replicaset.apps/my-deploy-8448c488b5       1         1         1       7m56s
```

Rendering Deployment Details

You can inspect the details of a Deployment using the `describe` command. Not only
does the output provide information on the number and availability of replicas, it
also presents you with the reference to the ReplicaSet. Inspecting the ReplicaSet or
the replicated Pods renders references to the parent object managing it:

```
$ kubectl describe deployment.apps/my-deploy
...
Replicas:               1 desired | 1 updated | 1 total | 1 available | \
                        0 unavailable
...
NewReplicaSet:   my-deploy-8448c488b5 (1/1 replicas created)
...
$ kubectl describe replicaset.apps/my-deploy-8448c488b5
....
Controlled By:  Deployment/my-deploy
....
$ kubectl describe pod/my-deploy-8448c488b5-mzx5g
....
Controlled By:  ReplicaSet/my-deploy-8448c488b5
....
```

Rolling Out a New Revision

Application development is usually not stagnant. As part of the software development lifecycle, you build a new feature or create a bug fix and deploy the changes to the Kubernetes cluster as part of the release process. In practice, you'd push a new Docker image to the registry bundling the changes so that they can be run in a container. By default, a Deployment rolls out a new container image using a zero-downtime strategy by updating Pods one by one. Figure 6-5 shows the rolling update process for a Deployment controlling two replicas from version 1.2.3 to 2.0.0.

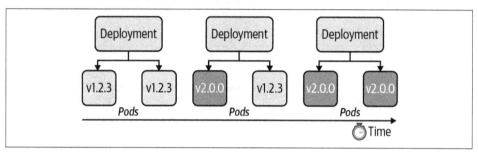

Figure 6-5. Rolling update of Pods managed by a Deployment

Every Deployment keeps a record of the rollout history. Within the history, a new version of a rollout is called a *revision*. Before experiencing the rollout of a new revision in practice, let's inspect the initial state of the Deployment named my-deploy. The rollout command shows revision 1, which represents the creation of the Deployment with all its settings:

```
$ kubectl rollout history deployment my-deploy
deployment.apps/my-deploy
REVISION   CHANGE-CAUSE
1          <none>
```

In the next step, we will update the container image used on the Deployment from nginx:1.14.2 to nginx:1.19.2. To do so, either edit the live object or run the set image command:

```
$ kubectl set image deployment my-deploy nginx=nginx:1.19.2
deployment.apps/my-deploy image updated
```

Looking at the rollout history again now shows revision 1 and 2. When changing the Pod template of a Deployment—for example, by updating the image—a new Replica-Set is created. The Deployment will gradually migrate the Pods from the old Replica-Set to the new one. Inspecting the Deployment details reveals a different name—in this case, my-deploy-775ccfcbc8:

```
$ kubectl rollout history deployment my-deploy
deployment.apps/my-deploy
```

```
REVISION   CHANGE-CAUSE
1          <none>
2          <none>
$ kubectl describe deployment.apps/my-deploy
...
NewReplicaSet:   my-deploy-775ccfcbc8 (1/1 replicas created)
...
$ kubectl rollout status deployment my-deploy
deployment "my-deploy" successfully rolled out
```

 By default, a Deployment persists a maximum of 10 revisions in its history. You can change the limit by assigning a different value to `spec.revisionHistoryLimit`.

You can also retrieve detailed information about a revision with the `rollout history` command by providing the revision number using the `--revision` command-line option. The details of a revision can give you an indication of *what exactly* changed between revisions:

```
$ kubectl rollout history deployments my-deploy --revision=2
deployment.apps/my-deploy with revision #2
Pod Template:
  Labels:       app=my-deploy
        pod-template-hash=9df7d9c6
  Containers:
   nginx:
    Image:      nginx:1.19.2
    Port:       <none>
    Host Port:  <none>
    Environment:        <none>
    Mounts:     <none>
  Volumes:      <none>
```

The rolling update strategy ensures that the application is always available to end users. This approach implies that two versions of the same application are available during the update process. As an application developer, you have to be aware that convenience doesn't come without potential side effects. If you happen to introduce a breaking change to the public API of your application, you might temporarily break consumers, as they could hit revision 1 or 2 of the application. You can change the default update strategy of a Deployment by providing a different value to the attribute `strategy.type`; however, consider the trade-offs. For example, the value `Recreate` kills all Pods first, then creates new Pods with the latest revision, causing a potential downtime for consumers. Other strategies like blue-green or canary deployments can be set up, though their coverage goes beyond the scope of the book.

Rolling Back to a Previous Revision

Despite the best efforts to avoid them by writing extensive test suites, bugs happen. Not only can the `rollout` command deploy a new version of an application, you can also roll back to an earlier revision. In the previous section, we rolled out revisions 1 and 2. Assume revision 2 contains a bug and we need to quickly revert to revision 1. The following command demonstrates the process:

```
$ kubectl rollout undo deployment my-deploy --to-revision=1
deployment.apps/my-deploy rolled back
```

If you look at the rollout history, you'll find revisions 2 and 3. Kubernetes recognizes that revisions 1 and 3 are exactly the same. For that reason, the rollout history deduplicates revision 1 effectively; revision 1 became revision 3:

```
$ kubectl rollout history deployment my-deploy
deployment.apps/my-deploy
REVISION   CHANGE-CAUSE
2          <none>
3          <none>
```

The rollback process works pretty much the same way as rolling out a new revision. Kubernetes switches back to the "old" ReplicaSet, drains the Pods with the image `nginx:1.19.2`, and starts new Pods with the image `nginx:1.14.2`.

Manually Scaling a Deployment

The scaling process is completely abstracted from the end user. You just have to tell the Deployment that you want to scale to a specified number of replicas. Kubernetes will take care of the rest.

Say we wanted to scale from one replica to five replicas, as shown in Figure 6-6.

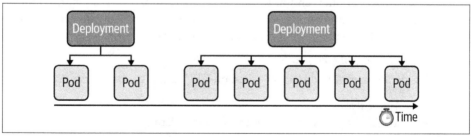

Figure 6-6. Scaling a Deployment

We have two options: using the `scale` command or changing the value of the `replicas` attribute for the live object. The following set of commands show the effect of scaling up a Deployment:

```
$ kubectl scale deployment my-deploy --replicas=5
deployment.apps/my-deploy scaled
$ kubectl get pods
NAME                             READY    STATUS              RESTARTS   AGE
my-deploy-8448c488b5-5f5tg       0/1      ContainerCreating   0          4s
my-deploy-8448c488b5-9xplx       0/1      ContainerCreating   0          4s
my-deploy-8448c488b5-d8q4t       0/1      ContainerCreating   0          4s
my-deploy-8448c488b5-f5kkm       0/1      ContainerCreating   0          4s
my-deploy-8448c488b5-mzx5g       1/1      Running             0          3d19h
$ kubectl get pods
NAME                             READY    STATUS     RESTARTS   AGE
my-deploy-8448c488b5-5f5tg       1/1      Running    0          44s
my-deploy-8448c488b5-9xplx       1/1      Running    0          44s
my-deploy-8448c488b5-d8q4t       1/1      Running    0          44s
my-deploy-8448c488b5-f5kkm       1/1      Running    0          44s
my-deploy-8448c488b5-mzx5g       1/1      Running    0          3d19h
$ kubectl get replicasets
NAME                    DESIRED    CURRENT    READY    AGE
my-deploy-8448c488b5    5          5          5        3d19h
```

A Deployment records scaling activities in its events, which we can view using the describe deployment command:

```
$ kubectl describe deployment.apps/my-deploy
...
Events:
  Type     Reason            Age     From                   Message
  ----     ------            ----    ----                   -------
  Normal   ScalingReplicaSet 4m42s   deployment-controller  Scaled up replica set \
                                                            my-deploy-8448c488b5 to 5
```

Autoscaling a Deployment

Scaling a Deployment based on the expected load requires manual supervision via monitoring or manual intervention by changing the number of replicas. Kubernetes offers primitives for taking on this job in an automated fashion: so-called autoscalers. On the level of a Deployment, we can differentiate two types of autoscalers:

Horizontal Pod Autoscaler (HPA)
   Scales the number of Pod replicas based on CPU and memory thresholds.

Vertical Pod Autoscaler (VPA)
   Scales the CPU and memory allocation for existing Pods based on historic metrics.

Both autoscalers use the metrics server we discussed in Chapter 5, *Observability*. Refer to the instructions on installing and enabling metrics support. Here, we will discuss how to create an autoscaler, but we won't go into details that demonstrate the practical behavior of those autoscalers under load. The Kubernetes documentation provides some practical scenarios to emulate real-world behavior under increased load.

The HPA is a standard feature of Kubernetes, whereas the VPA has to the supported by your cloud provider as an add-on or needs to be installed manually. Therefore, only the HPA will be relevant to the CKAD exam. To learn more, check your provider's documentation or the GitHub repository kubernetes/autoscaler (*https://oreil.ly/ GRmyo*).

Horizontal Pod Autoscaler

Figure 6-7 shows the use of an HPA that will scale up the number of replicas if an average of 70% CPU utilization is reached across all available Pods controlled by the Deployment.

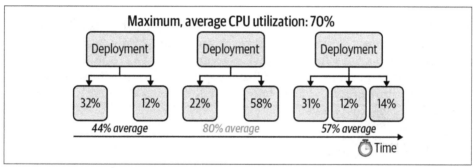

Figure 6-7. Autoscaling a Deployment horizontally

A Deployment can be autoscaled using the `autoscale deployment` command. Provide the name and the thresholds you'd like the autoscaler to act upon. In the following example, we're specifying a minimum of 2 replicas at any given time, a maximum number of 8 replicas the HPA can scale up to, and the CPU utilization threshold of 70%. Listing the HPAs in the namespace reflects those numbers. You can use the primitive name `horizontalpodautoscalers` for the command; however, I prefer the short-form notation `hpa`:

```
$ kubectl autoscale deployment my-deploy --cpu-percent=70 --min=2 --max=8
horizontalpodautoscaler.autoscaling/my-deploy autoscaled
$ kubectl get hpa
NAME        REFERENCE              TARGETS        MINPODS  MAXPODS  REPLICAS  AGE
my-deploy   Deployment/my-deploy   <unknown>/70%  2        8        2         37s
```

The current status of the HPA shows the upper CPU threshold limit but renders `<unknown>` for the current CPU consumption. That's usually the case if the metrics server is not running, is misconfigured, or if the Pod template of the Deployment doesn't define any resource requirements. Check the events of the HPA using the command `kubectl describe hpa my-deploy`.

What you should usually see is a percentage number to indicate the current CPU utilization, as shown in the following terminal output. None of the Pods consumes CPU resources at the time of querying the information:

```
$ kubectl describe hpa my-deploy
Name:                                              my-deploy
...
Reference:                                         Deployment/my-deploy
Metrics:                                           ( current / target )
  resource cpu on pods  (as a percentage of request):  0% (0) / 70%
Min replicas:                                      3
Max replicas:                                      8
Deployment pods:                                   3 current / 3 desired
...
```

The API spec `autoscaling/v1` only supports autoscaling capabilities based on CPU utilization. The new API spec version `autoscaling/v2beta2` provides a more generic approach to defining metric thresholds. For example, you can specify a scaling threshold for memory consumption. Given that the specification is still in its beta state, we won't cover it in more detail here; refer to the Kubernetes documentation (*https://oreil.ly/Ce_xE*) for more information.

Understanding Jobs

A Pod is meant for the continuous operation of an application. You will want to deploy the application with a specific version and then keep it running without interrupts if possible.

A Job is a Kubernetes primitive with a different goal. It runs functionality until a specified number of completions has been reached, making it a good fit for one-time operations like import/export data processes or I/O-intensive processes with a finite end. The actual work managed by a Job is still running inside of a Pod. Therefore, you can think of a Job as a higher-level coordination instance for Pods executing the workload.

Upon completion of a Job and its Pods, Kubernetes does not automatically delete the objects—they will stay until they're explicity deleted. Keeping those objects helps with debugging the command run inside of the Pod and gives you a chance to inspect the logs.

Kubernetes supports an auto-cleanup mechanism for Jobs and their controlled Pods by specifying the attribute `spec.ttlSecondsAfterFinished`. Be aware that the feature is still in an alpha state and needs to be enabled explicitly for a cluster by setting a feature flag.

Creating and Inspecting Jobs

Let's first create a Job and see its behavior in practice before delving into any details. To create a Job imperatively, simply use the create job command. If the provided image doesn't run any commands, you may want to append a command to be executed in the corresponding Pod. The following command creates a Job that runs an iteration process. For each iteration of the loop, a variable named counter is incremented. The command execution finishes after reaching the counter value 3:

```
$ kubectl create job counter --image=nginx -- /bin/sh -c 'counter=0; \
  while [ $counter -lt 3 ]; do counter=$((counter+1)); echo "$counter"; \
  sleep 3; done;'
job.batch/counter created
```

The output of listing the Job shows the current number of completions and the expected number of completions. The default number of completions is 1. This means if the Pod executing the command was successful, a Job is considered completed. As you can see in the following terminal output, a Job uses a single Pod by default to perform the work. The corresponding Pod can be identified by name—it uses the Job name as a prefix in its own name:

```
$ kubectl get jobs
NAME        COMPLETIONS   DURATION   AGE
counter     0/1           13s        13s
$ kubectl get jobs
NAME        COMPLETIONS   DURATION   AGE
counter     1/1           15s        19s
$ kubectl get pods
NAME            READY   STATUS      RESTARTS   AGE
counter-z6kdj   0/1     Completed   0          51s
```

To verify the correct behavior of the Job, you can download the logs of the Pod. As expected, the output renders the counter for each iteration:

```
$ kubectl logs counter-z6kdj
1
2
3
```

If you'd rather go the declarative route by creating a YAML manifest, the following code snippet shown in Example 6-4.

Example 6-4. A Job executing a loop command

```
apiVersion: batch/v1
kind: Job
metadata:
  name: counter
spec:
  template:
```

```
spec:
  containers:
  - name: counter
    image: nginx
    command:
    - /bin/sh
    - -c
    - counter=0; while [ $counter -lt 3 ]; do counter=$((counter+1)); \
      echo "$counter"; sleep 3; done;
    restartPolicy: Never
```

Job Operation Types

The default behavior of a Job is to run the workload in a single Pod and expect one successful completion. That's what Kubernetes calls a *non-parallel* Job. Internally, those parameters are tracked by the attributes spec.template.spec.completions and spec.template.spec.parallelism, each with the assigned value 1. The following command renders the parameters of the Job we created earlier:

```
$ kubectl get jobs counter -o yaml | grep -C 1 "completions"
...
  completions: 1
  parallelism: 1
...
```

You can tweak any of those parameters to fit the needs of your use case. Say you'd expect the workload to complete successfully multiple times; then you'd increase the value of spec.template.spec.completions to at least 2. Sometimes, you'll want to execute the workload by multiple pods in parallel. In those cases, you'd bump up the value assigned to spec.template.spec.parallelism. This is referred to as a *parallel job*. Remember that you can use any combination of assigned values for both attributes. Table 6-1 summarizes the different use cases.

Table 6-1. Configuration for different Job operation types

Type	spec.completions	spec.parallelism	Description
Non-parallel with one completion count	1	1	Completes as soon as its Pod terminates successfully.
Parallel with a fixed completion count	>= 1	>= 1	Completes when specified number of tasks finish successfully.
Parallel with worker queue	unset	>= 1	Completes when at least one Pod has terminated successfully and all Pods are terminated.

Restart Behavior

The `spec.backoffLimit` attribute determines the number of retries a Job attempts to successfully complete the workload until the executed command finishes with an exit code 0. The default is 6, which means it will execute the workload 6 times before the Job is considered unsuccessful.

The Job manifest needs to explicitly declare the restart policy by using `spec.template.spec.restartPolicy`. The default restart policy of a Pod is `Always`, which tells the Kubernetes scheduler to *always* restart the Pod even if the container exits with a zero exit code. The restart policy of a Job can only be `OnFailure` or `Never`.

Restarting the Container on Failure

Figure 6-8 shows the behavior of a Job that uses the restart policy `OnFailure`. Upon a container failure, this policy will simply rerun the container.

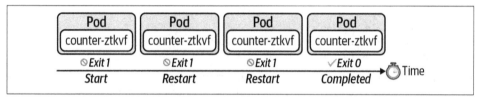

Figure 6-8. Restart policy onFailure

Starting a New Pod on Failure

Figure 6-9 shows the behavior of a Job that uses the restart policy `Never`. This policy does not restart the container upon a failure. It starts a new Pod instead.

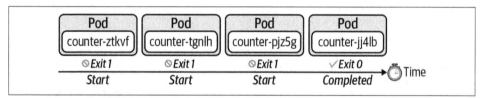

Figure 6-9. Restart policy Never

Understanding CronJobs

A Job represents a finite operation. Once the operation could be executed successfully, the work is done and the Job will create no more Pods. A CronJob is essentially a Job, but it's run periodically based a schedule; however, it will continue to create a new Pod when it's time to run the task. The schedule can be defined with a cron-expression you may already know from Unix cron jobs. Figure 6-10 shows a CronJob that executes every hour. For every execution, the CronJob creates a new Pod that runs the task and finishes with a zero or non-zero exit code.

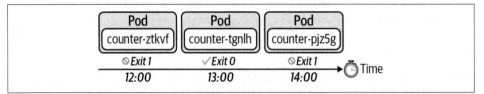

Figure 6-10. Executing a Job based on a schedule

Creating and Inspecting Jobs

You can use the imperative `create cronjob` command to create a new CronJob. The following command schedules the CronJob to run every minute. The Pod created for every execution renders the current date to standard output using the Unix `echo` command:

```
$ kubectl create cronjob current-date --schedule="* * * * *" --image=nginx \
   -- /bin/sh -c 'echo "Current date: $(date)"'
cronjob.batch/current-date created
```

If you list the existing CronJob with the `get cronjobs` command, you will see the schedule, the last scheduled execution, and whether the CronJob is currently active. It's easy to match Pods managed by a CronJob. You can simply identify them by the name prefix. In this case, the prefix is `current-date-`:

```
$ kubectl get cronjobs
NAME            SCHEDULE     SUSPEND   ACTIVE   LAST SCHEDULE   AGE
current-date    * * * * *    False     0        <none>>         28s
$ kubectl get cronjobs
NAME            SCHEDULE     SUSPEND   ACTIVE   LAST SCHEDULE   AGE
current-date    * * * * *    False     1        14s             53s
$ kubectl get cronjobs
NAME            SCHEDULE     SUSPEND   ACTIVE   LAST SCHEDULE   AGE
current-date    * * * * *    False     0        19s             58s
$ kubectl get pods
NAME                         READY   STATUS             RESTARTS   AGE
current-date-1598651700-2xgn9  0/1   Completed          0          63s
current-date-1598651760-rt6c6  0/1   ContainerCreating  0          1s
```

To create a CronJob from the YAML manifest, start with the definition in Example 6-5 and tweak as needed.

Example 6-5. A CronJob printing the current date

```
apiVersion: batch/v1beta1
kind: CronJob
metadata:
```

```
    name: current-date
spec:
  schedule: "* * * * *"
  jobTemplate:
    spec:
      template:
        spec:
          containers:
          - name: current-date
            image: nginx
            args:
            - /bin/sh
            - -c
            - 'echo "Current date: $(date)"'
          restartPolicy: OnFailure
```

Configuring Retained Job History

Even after completing a task in a Pod controlled by a CronJob, it will not be deleted
automatically. Keeping a historical record of Pods can be tremendously helpful for
troubleshooting failed workloads or inspecting the logs. By default, a CronJob retains
the last three successful Pods and the last failed Pod:

```
$ kubectl get cronjobs current-date -o yaml | grep successfulJobsHistoryLimit:
  successfulJobsHistoryLimit: 3
$ kubectl get cronjobs current-date -o yaml | grep failedJobsHistoryLimit:
  failedJobsHistoryLimit: 1
```

In order to reconfigure the job retention history limits, set new values for the
attributes `spec.successfulJobsHistoryLimit` and `spec.failedJobsHistoryLimit`.
Example 6-6 keeps the last five successful executions and the last three failed
executions.

Example 6-6. A CronJob configuring retention history limits

```
apiVersion: batch/v1beta1
kind: CronJob
metadata:
  name: current-date
spec:
  successfulJobsHistoryLimit: 5
  failedJobsHistoryLimit: 3
  schedule: "* * * * *"
  jobTemplate:
    spec:
      template:
        spec:
          containers:
          - name: current-date
            image: nginx
```

```
      args:
      - /bin/sh
      - -c
      - 'echo "Current date: $(date)"'
    restartPolicy: OnFailure
```

Summary

Labels are one of the central concepts that control the runtime behavior of more advanced Kubernetes objects. For example, in the context of a Deployment, label selection is used to *select* the Pods the Deployment manages. You can use labels to select objects based on a query from the command line or within a manifest if supported by the primitive's API. Annotations serve a different purpose—they are only meant for providing human-readable, informative metadata and can be used for querying objects.

The Deployment is an essential primitive for scaling an application by running it in multiple replicas. The heavy lifting of managing those replicas is performed by a ReplicaSet. Application developers do not have to interact directly with the ReplicaSet; a Deployment handles it under the hood. Deployments come with the capability to easily roll out and roll back revisions of the application represented by an image running in the container. You learned about the commands for controlling the revision history and its operations. Scaling a Deployment manually requires deep insight into the requirements and the load of an application. A Horizontal Pod Autoscaler can automatically scale the number of replicas based on CPU and memory thresholds observed at runtime.

Jobs are well suited for implementing batch processes run in one or many Pods as a finite operation. Both objects, the Job and the Pod, will not be deleted after the work is completed in order to support inspection and troubleshooting activities. A CronJob is very similar to a Job, but executes on a schedule, defined as a Unix cron expression.

Exam Essentials

Understand the difference between labels and annotations

Labels are an extremely important concept in Kubernetes, as many other primitives work with label selection. Practice how to declare labels for different objects, and use the -l command-line option to query for them based on equality-based and set-based requirements. Label selection in a YAML manifest may look slightly different depending on the API version of the spec. Confront yourself with the use of label selection for primitives that make heavy use of them. All you need to know about annotations is their declaration from the command line and in a YAML manifest.

Know the ins and outs of a Deployment

Given that a Deployment is such a central primitive in Kubernetes, you can almost be certain that the exam will test you on it. Know how to create a Deployment and learn how to scale to multiple replicas. One of the superior features of a Deployment is its rollout functionality of new revisions. Practice how to roll out a new revision, inspect the rollout history, and roll back to a previous revision. It won't hurt to also get more familiar with auto-scaling a Deployment using the Horizontal Pod Autoscaler.

Understand practical use cases of Jobs and CronJobs

Jobs and CronJobs manage Pods that should finish the work at least once or periodically. You will need to understand the creation of those objects and how to inspect them at runtime. Make sure to play around with the different configuration options and how they effect the runtime behavior.

Sample Exercises

Solutions to these exercises are available in the Appendix.

1. Create three Pods that use the image `nginx`. The names of the Pods should be `pod-1`, `pod-2`, and `pod-3`. Assign the label `tier=frontend` to `pod-1` and the label `tier=backend` to `pod-2` and `pod-3`. All pods should also assign the label `team=artemidis`.

2. Assign the annotation with the key `deployer` to `pod-1` and `pod-3`. Use your own name as the value.

3. From the command line, use label selection to find all Pods with the team `artemidis` or `aircontrol` and that are considered a backend service.

4. Create a new Deployment named `server-deployment`. The Deployment should control two replicas using the image `grand-server:1.4.6`.

5. Inspect the Deployment and find out the root cause for its failure.

6. Fix the issue by assigning the image `nginx` instead. Inspect the rollout history. How many revisions would you expect to see?

7. Create a new CronJob named `google-ping`. When executed, the Job should run a `curl` command for `google.com`. Pick an appropriate image. The excution should occur every two minutes.

8. Tail the logs of the CronJob at runtime. Check the command-line options of the relevant command or consult the Kubernetes documentation.

9. Reconfigure the CronJob to retain a history of seven executions.

10. Reconfigure the CronJob to disallow a new execution if the current execution is still running. Consult the Kubernetes documentation for more information.

## CHAPTER 7

Services & Networking

In Chapter 2, *Core Concepts*, we learned that you can communicate with a Pod by targeting its IP address. It's important to recognize that Pods' IP addresses are virtual and will therefore change to random values over time. A restart of a Pod will automatically assign a new virtual cluster IP address. Therefore, other parts of your system cannot rely on the Pod's IP address if they need to talk to one another.

The Kubernetes primitive Service implements an abstraction layer on top of Pods, assigning a fixed virtual IP fronting all the Pods with matching labels, and that virtual IP is called Cluster IP. This chapter will focus on the ins and outs of Services, and most importantly the exposure of Pods inside or outside of the cluster depending on their declared type.

By default, Kubernetes does not restrict inter-Pod communication in any shape or form. You can define a network policy to mitigate potential security risks. Network policies describe the access rules for incoming and outgoing network traffic to and from Pods. By the end of this chapter, you will have a basic understanding of its functionality based on common use cases.

At a high level, this chapter covers the following concepts:

- Service
- Deployment
- Network Policy

Understanding Services

Services are one of the central concepts in Kubernetes. Without a Service, you won't be able to expose your application to consumers in a stable and predictable fashion.

In a nutshell, Services provide discoverable names and load balancing to Pod replicas. The services and Pods remain agnostic from IPs with the help of the Kubernetes DNS control plane component. Similar to a Deployment, the Service determines the Pods it works on with the help of label selection.

Figure 7-1 illustrates the functionality. Pod 1 and Pod 2 receive traffic, as their assigned labels match with the label selection defined in the Service. Pod 3 does not receive traffic, as it defines non-matching labels. Note that it is possible to create a Service without a label selector for less-common scenarios. Refer to the relevant Kubernetes documentation (*https://oreil.ly/30PzS*) for more information.

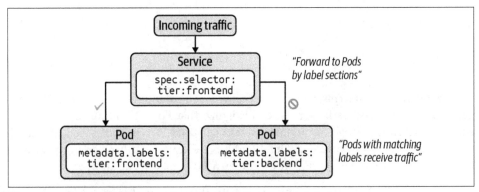

Figure 7-1. Service routing traffic to Pods with matching labels

Service Types

Every Service needs to define a type. The type determines how the Service exposes the matching Pods, as listed in Table 7-1.

Table 7-1. Service types

Type	Description
ClusterIP	Exposes the Service on a cluster-internal IP. Only reachable from within the cluster.
NodePort	Exposes the Service on each node's IP address at a static port. Accessible from outside of the cluster.
LoadBalancer	Exposes the Service externally using a cloud provider's load balancer.
ExternalName	Maps a Service to a DNS name.

The most important types you will need to understand for the CKAD exam are ClusterIP and NodePort. Those types make Pods reachable from within the cluster and from outside of the cluster. Later in this chapter, we'll explore both types by example.

Creating Services

As usual, we'll look at creating a Service from both the imperative and declarative approach angles. In fact, there are two ways to create a Service imperatively.

The command `create service` instantiates a new Service. You have to provide the type of the Service as the third, mandatory command-line option. That's also the case for the default type, `ClusterIP`. In addition, you can optionally provide the port mapping, which we'll discuss a little later in this chapter:

```
$ kubectl create service clusterip nginx-service --tcp=80:80
service/nginx-service created
```

Instead of creating a Service as a standalone object, you can also *expose* a Pod or Deployment with a single command. The `run` command provides an optional `--expose` command-line option, which creates a new Pod and a corresponding Service with the correct label selection in place:

```
$ kubectl run nginx --image=nginx --restart=Never --port=80 --expose
service/nginx created
pod/nginx created
```

For an existing Deployment, you can expose the underlying Pods with a Service using the `expose deployment` command:

```
$ kubectl expose deployment my-deploy --port=80 --target-port=80
service/my-deploy exposed
```

The `expose` command and the `--expose` command-line option are welcome shortcuts as a means to creating a new Service during the CKAD exam with a fast turnaround time.

Using the declarative approach, you would define a Service manifest in YAML form as shown in Example 7-1. As you can see, the key of the label selector uses the value `app`. After creating the Service, you will likely have to change the label selection criteria to meet your needs, as the `create service` command does not offer a dedicated command-line option for it.

Example 7-1. A Service defined by a YAML manifest

```
apiVersion: v1
kind: Service
metadata:
  name: nginx-service
spec:
  type: ClusterIP
  selector:
    app: nginx-service
  ports:
```

```
  - port: 80
    targetPort: 80
```

Listing Services

You can observe the most important attributes of a Service when rendering the full list for a namespace. The following command shows the type, the cluster IP, an optional external IP, and the mapped ports:

```
$ kubectl get services
NAME            TYPE        CLUSTER-IP       EXTERNAL-IP   PORT(S)   AGE
nginx-service   ClusterIP   10.109.125.232   <none>        80/TCP    82m
```

Rendering Service Details

The describe command helps with retrieving even more details about a Service. The label selector will be included in the description of the Service, represented by the attribute Selector. That's important information when troubleshooting a Service object:

```
$ kubectl describe service nginx-service
Name:              nginx-service
Namespace:         default
Labels:            app=nginx-service
Annotations:       <none>
Selector:          app=nginx-service
Type:              ClusterIP
IP:                10.109.125.232
Port:              80-80  80/TCP
TargetPort:        80/TCP
Endpoints:         <none>
Session Affinity:  None
Events:            <none>
```

Port Mapping

In "Creating Services" on page 113, we only briefly touched on the topic of port mapping. The correct port mapping determines if the incoming traffic actually reaches the application running inside of the Pods that match the label selection criteria of the Service. A Service always defines two different ports: the incoming port accepting traffic and the outgoing port, also called the target port. Their functionality is best illustrated by example.

Figure 7-2 shows a Service that accepts incoming traffic on port 3000. That's the port defined by the attribute ports.port in the manifest. Any incoming traffic is then routed toward the target port, represented by ports.targetPort. The target port is the same port as defined by the container running inside of the label-selected Pod. In this case, that's port 80.

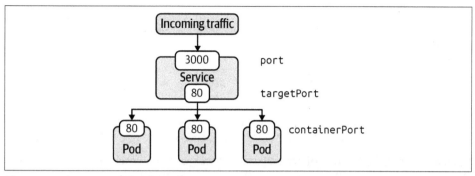

Figure 7-2. Port mapping of a Service to a Pod

Accessing a Service with Type ClusterIP

ClusterIP is the default type of Service. It exposes the Service on a cluster-internal IP address. Figure 7-3 shows how to reach a Pod exposed by the ClusterIP type from another Pod from within the cluster. You can also create a proxy from outside of the cluster using the kubectl proxy command. Using a proxy is not only meant for production environments but can also be helpful for troubleshooting a Service.

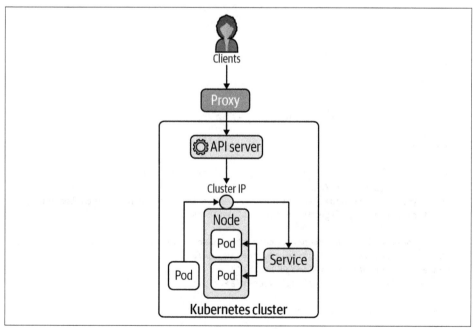

Figure 7-3. Accessibility of a Service with the type ClusterIP

To demonstrate the use case, we'll opt for a quick way to create the Pod and the corresponding Service with the same command. The command automatically takes care of properly mapping labels and ports:

```
$ kubectl run nginx --image=nginx --restart=Never --port=80 --expose
service/nginx created
pod/nginx created
$ kubectl get pod,service
NAME        READY   STATUS    RESTARTS   AGE
pod/nginx   1/1     Running   0          26s

NAME            TYPE        CLUSTER-IP      EXTERNAL-IP   PORT(S)   AGE
service/nginx   ClusterIP   10.96.225.204   <none>        80/TCP    26s
```

Remember that the Service of type `ClusterIP` can only be reached from within the cluster. To demonstrate the behavior, we'll create a new Pod running in the same cluster and execute a `wget` command to access the application. Have a look at the cluster IP exposed by the Service—that's `10.96.225.204`. The port is 80. Combined as a single command, you can resolve the application via `wget -O- 10.96.225.204:80` from the temporary Pod:

```
$ kubectl run busybox --image=busybox --restart=Never -it -- /bin/sh
If you don't see a command prompt, try pressing enter.
/ # wget -O- 10.96.225.204:80
Connecting to 10.96.225.204:80 (10.96.225.204:80)
writing to stdout
<!DOCTYPE html>
<html>
<head>
<title>Welcome to nginx!</title>
<style>
    body {
        width: 35em;
        margin: 0 auto;
        font-family: Tahoma, Verdana, Arial, sans-serif;
    }
</style>
</head>
<body>
<h1>Welcome to nginx!</h1>
<p>If you see this page, the nginx web server is successfully installed and \
working. Further configuration is required.</p>

<p>For online documentation and support please refer to
<a href="http://nginx.org/">nginx.org</a>.<br/>
Commercial support is available at
<a href="http://nginx.com/">nginx.com</a>.</p>

<p><em>Thank you for using nginx.</em></p>
</body>
</html>
```

```
-                    100% |************************************************ \
*********************|   612  0:00:00 ETA
written to stdout
/ # exit
```

The `proxy` command can establish a direct connection to the Kubernetes API server from your localhost. With the following command, we are opening port 9999 on which to run the proxy:

```
$ kubectl proxy --port=9999
Starting to serve on 127.0.0.1:9999
```

After running the command, you will notice that the shell is going to wait until you break out of the operation. To try talking to the proxy, you will have to open another terminal window. Say you have the `curl` command-line tool installed on your machine to make a call to an endpoint of the API server. The following example uses `localhost:9999`—that's the proxy entry point. As part of the URL, you're providing the endpoint to the Service named `nginx` running in the `default` namespace according to the API reference (*https://oreil.ly/7pFBX*):

```
$ curl -L localhost:9999/api/v1/namespaces/default/services/nginx/proxy
<!DOCTYPE html>
<html>
<head>
<title>Welcome to nginx!</title>
<style>
    body {
        width: 35em;
        margin: 0 auto;
        font-family: Tahoma, Verdana, Arial, sans-serif;
    }
</style>
</head>
<body>
<h1>Welcome to nginx!</h1>
<p>If you see this page, the nginx web server is successfully installed and \
working. Further configuration is required.</p>

<p>For online documentation and support please refer to
<a href="http://nginx.org/">nginx.org</a>.<br/>
Commercial support is available at
<a href="http://nginx.com/">nginx.com</a>.</p>

<p><em>Thank you for using nginx.</em></p>
</body>
</html>
```

Accessing a Service with Type NodePort

Declaring a Service with type NodePort exposes access through the node's IP address and can be resolved from outside of the Kubernetes cluster. The node's IP address can be reached in combination with a port number in the range of 30000 and 32767, assigned automatically upon the creation of the Service. Figure 7-4 illustrates the routing of traffic to Pods via a NodePort-typed Service.

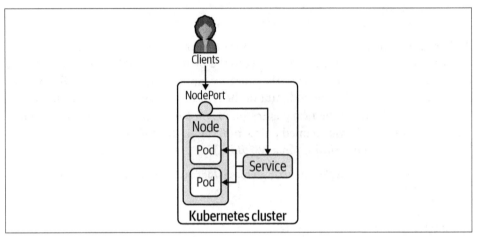

Figure 7-4. Accessibility of a Service with the type NodePort

Let's enhance the example from the previous section. We'll change the existing Service named nginx to use the type NodePort instead of ClusterIP. There are various ways to implement the change. For this example, we'll use the patch command. When listing the Service, you will find the changed type and the port you can use to reach the Service. The port that has been assigned in this example is 32300:

```
$ kubectl patch service nginx -p '{ "spec": {"type": "NodePort"} }'
service/nginx patched
$ kubectl get service nginx
NAME    TYPE        CLUSTER-IP      EXTERNAL-IP    PORT(S)       AGE
nginx   NodePort    10.96.225.204   <none>         80:32300/TCP  3d21h
```

You should now be able to access the Service using the node IP address and the node port. One way to discover the IP address of the node is by first listing all available nodes and then inspecting the relevant ones for details. In the following commands, we are only running on a single-node Kubernetes cluster, which makes things easy:

```
$ kubectl get nodes
NAME       STATUS   ROLES    AGE   VERSION
minikube   Ready    master   91d   v1.18.3
$ kubectl describe node minikube | grep InternalIP:
  InternalIP:  192.168.64.2
$ curl 192.168.64.2:32300
```

```
<!DOCTYPE html>
<html>
<head>
<title>Welcome to nginx!</title>
<style>
    body {
        width: 35em;
        margin: 0 auto;
        font-family: Tahoma, Verdana, Arial, sans-serif;
    }
</style>
</head>
<body>
<h1>Welcome to nginx!</h1>
<p>If you see this page, the nginx web server is successfully installed and \
working. Further configuration is required.</p>

<p>For online documentation and support please refer to
<a href="http://nginx.org/">nginx.org</a>.<br/>
Commercial support is available at
<a href="http://nginx.com/">nginx.co</a>.</p>

<p><em>Thank you for using nginx.</em></p>
</body>
</html>
```

Deployments and Services

In this chapter, we discussed the primitive Service in detail. Many tutorials and examples on the internet explain the concept of a Service in conjunction with a Deployment. I'm sure it became abundantly clear that a Service does not need a Deployment to work *but* they can work in tandem, as shown in Figure 7-5. A Deployment manages Pods and their replication. A Service routes network requests to a set of Pods. Both primitives use label selection to connect with an associated set of Pods.

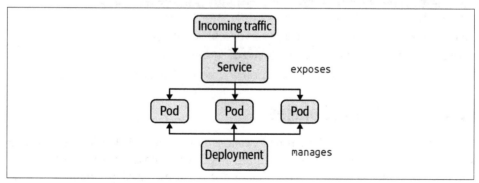

Figure 7-5. Relationship between a Deployment and Service

Understanding Network Policies

Within a Kubernetes cluster, any Pod can talk to any other Pod without restrictions using its IP address or DNS name (*https://oreil.ly/tllLY*), even across namespaces. Not only does unrestricted inter-Pod communication pose a potential security risk, it also makes it harder to understand the mental communication model of your architecture. For example, there's no good reason to allow a backend application running in a Pod to directly talk to the frontend application running in another Pod. The communication should be directed from the frontend Pod to the backend Pod. A network policy defines the rules that control traffic from and to a Pod, as illustrated in Figure 7-6.

Figure 7-6. Network policies define traffic from and to a Pod

Label selection plays a crucial role in defining which Pods a network policy applies to. We already saw the concept in action in other contexts (e.g., the Deployment and the Service). Furthermore, a network policy defines the direction of the traffic, to allow or disallow. Incoming traffic is called *ingress*, and outgoing traffic is called *egress*. For ingress and egress, you can whitelist the sources of traffic like Pods, IP addresses, or ports.

A network policy defines a couple of important attributes, which together forms its set of rules. I want to discuss them first in Table 7-2, before looking at an exemplary scenario, so you have a rough idea what they mean in essence.

Table 7-2. Configuration elements of a network policy

Attribute	Description
podSelector	Selects the Pods in the namespace to apply the network policy to.
policyTypes	Defines the type of traffic (i.e., ingress and/or egress) the network policy applies to.
ingress	Lists the rules for incoming traffic. Each rule can define from and ports sections.
egress	Lists the rules for outgoing traffic. Each rule can define to and ports sections.

Creating Network Policies

The creation of network policies is best explained by example. Let's say you're dealing with the following scenario: you're running a Pod that exposes an API to other consumers. For example, it's a Pod that handles the processing of payments for other applications. The company you're working for is in the process of migrating applications from a legacy payment processor to a new one. Therefore, you'll only want to allow access from the applications that are capable of properly communicating with it. Right now, you have two consumers—a grocery store and a coffee shop—each running their application in a separate Pod. The coffee shop is ready to consume the API of payment processor, but the grocery store isn't. Figure 7-7 shows the Pods and their assigned labels.

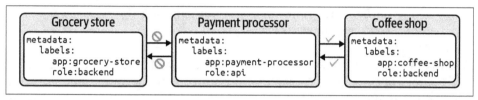

Figure 7-7. Limiting traffic to and from a Pod

You cannot create a new network policy with the imperative `create` command. Instead, you will have to use the declarative approach. The YAML manifest in Example 7-2, stored in the file *networkpolicy-api-allow.yaml*, shows a network policy for the scenario described previously.

Example 7-2. Declaring a NetworkPolicy with YAML

```
apiVersion: networking.k8s.io/v1
kind: NetworkPolicy
metadata:
  name: api-allow
spec:
  podSelector:
    matchLabels:
      app: payment-processor
      role: api
  ingress:
  - from:
    - podSelector:
        matchLabels:
          app: coffeeshop
```

Before creating the network policy, you'll stand up the Pod that runs the payment processor:

```
$ kubectl run payment-processor --image=nginx --restart=Never \
  -l app=payment-processor,role=api --port 80
pod/payment-processor created
$ kubectl get pods -o wide
NAME                READY STATUS  RESTARTS AGE    IP        NODE     NOMINATED NODE \
  READINESS GATES
payment-processor 1/1   Running 0        6m43s 10.0.0.51 minikube <none> \
  <none>
$ kubectl create -f networkpolicy-api-allow.yaml
networkpolicy.networking.k8s.io/api-allow created
```

Without a network policy controller, network policies won't have any effect. You need to configure a network overlay solution that provides this controller. If you're testing network policies on minikube, you'll have to go through some extra steps to install and enable the network provider Cilium. Without adhering to the proper prerequisites, network policies won't have any effect. You can find guidance on a dedicated page (*https://oreil.ly/ac47S*) in the Kubernetes documentation.

To verify the correct behavior of the network policy, you'll emulate the grocery store Pod and the coffeshop Pod. As you can see in the following console output, traffic from the grocery store Pod is blocked:

```
$ kubectl run grocery-store --rm -it --image=busybox \
  --restart=Never -l app=grocery-store,role=backend -- /bin/sh
/ # wget --spider --timeout=1 10.0.0.51
Connecting to 10.0.0.51 (10.0.0.51:80)
wget: download timed out
/ # exit
pod "grocery-store" deleted
```

Accessing the payment processor from the coffeeshop Pod works perfectly, as the Pod selector matches the label app=coffeeshop:

```
$ kubectl run coffeeshop --rm -it --image=busybox \
  --restart=Never -l app=coffeeshop,role=backend -- /bin/sh
/ # wget --spider --timeout=1 10.0.0.51
Connecting to 10.0.0.51 (10.0.0.51:80)
remote file exists
/ # exit
pod "coffeshop" deleted
```

Listing Network Policies

Listing network policies works the same as any other Kubernetes primitive. Use the get command in combination with the resource type networkpolicy, or its short-form, netpol. For the previous network policy, you see a table that renders the name and Pod selector:

```
$ kubectl get networkpolicy
NAME          POD-SELECTOR                     AGE
api-allow     app=payment-processor,role=api   83m
```

It's unfortunate that the output of the command doesn't give away a lot of information about the rules. To retrieve more information, you have to dig into the details.

Rendering Network Policy Details

You can inspect the details of a network policy using the `describe` command. The output renders all the important information: Pod selector, and ingress and egress rules:

```
$ kubectl describe networkpolicy api-allow
Name:         api-allow
Namespace:    default
Created on:   2020-09-26 18:02:57 -0600 MDT
Labels:       <none>
Annotations:  <none>
Spec:
  PodSelector:     app=payment-processor,role=api
  Allowing ingress traffic:
    To Port: <any> (traffic allowed to all ports)
    From:
      PodSelector: app=coffeeshop
  Not affecting egress traffic
  Policy Types: Ingress
```

The network policy details don't draw a clear picture of the Pods that have been selected based on its rules. It would be extremely useful to be presented with a visual representation. The product Weave Cloud (*https://oreil.ly/5QTSn*) can provide such a visualization to make troubleshooting network policies easier. Remember that you do not have access to this product during the CKAD exam.

Isolating All Pods in a Namespace

The safest approach to writing a new network policy is to define it in a way that disallows all ingress and egress traffic. With those constraints in place, you can define more detailed rules and loosen restrictions gradually. The Kubernetes documentation describes such a default policy as shown in Example 7-3.

Example 7-3. Disallowing all traffic with the default policy

```
apiVersion: networking.k8s.io/v1
kind: NetworkPolicy
metadata:
  name: default-deny-all
spec:
  podSelector: {}
  policyTypes:
  - Ingress
  - Egress
```

The curly braces for `spec.podSelector` mean "apply to all Pods in the namespace." The attribute `spec.policyTypes` defines the types of traffic the rule should apply to.

We can easily verify the correct behavior. Say, we're dealing with a Pod serving up frontend logic and another Pod that provides the backend functionality. The backend functionality is a basic NGINX web server exposing its endpoint on port 80. First, we'll create the backend Pod and connect to it from the frontend Pod running the busybox image. We should have no problem connecting to the backend Pod:

```
$ kubectl run backend --image=nginx --restart=Never --port=80
pod/backend created
$ kubectl get pods backend -o wide
NAME       READY    STATUS     RESTARTS   AGE   IP          NODE        \
   NOMINATED NODE   READINESS GATES
backend    1/1      Running    0          16s   10.0.0.61   minikube \
   <none>           <none>
$ kubectl run frontend --rm -it --image=busybox --restart=Never -- /bin/sh
/ # wget --spider --timeout=1 10.0.0.61
Connecting to 10.0.0.61 (10.0.0.61:80)
remote file exists
/ # exit
pod "frontend" deleted
```

Now, we'll go through the same procedure but with the "deny all" network policy put in place. Ingress access to the backend Pod will be blocked:

```
$ kubectl create -f networkpolicy-deny-all.yaml
networkpolicy.networking.k8s.io/default-deny-all created
$ kubectl run frontend --rm -it --image=busybox --restart=Never -- /bin/sh
If you don't see a command prompt, try pressing enter.
/ # wget --spider --timeout=1 10.0.0.61
Connecting to 10.0.0.61 (10.0.0.61:80)
wget: download timed out
/ # exit
pod "frontend" deleted
```

Restricting Access to Ports

If not specified by a network policy, all ports are accessible. There are good reasons why you may want to restrict access on the port level as well. Say you're running an application in a Pod that only exposes port 8080 to the outside. While convenient during development, it widens the attack vector on any other port that's not relevant to the application. Port rules can be specified for ingress and egress as part of a network policy. The definition of a network policy in Example 7-4 allows access on port 8080.

Example 7-4. Definition of a network policy allowing ingress access on port 8080

```
apiVersion: networking.k8s.io/v1
kind: NetworkPolicy
metadata:
  name: port-allow
```

```
spec:
  podSelector:
    matchLabels:
      app: backend
  ingress:
  - from:
    - podSelector:
        matchLabels:
          app: frontend
    ports:
    - protocol: TCP
      port: 8080
```

Summary

Pod-to-Pod communication should be through a Service. Services provide networking rules for a select set of Pods. Any traffic routed through the Service will be forwarded to Pods. You can assign one of the following types to a Service: ClusterIP, the default type; NodePort; LoadBalancer; or ExternalName. The selected type determines how the Pods are made available—for example, only from within the cluster or accessible from outside of the cluster. In practice, you'll commonly see a Deployment and a Service working together, though they serve different purposes and can operate independently.

Intra-Pod communication or communication between two containers of the same Pod is completely unrestricted in Kubernetes. Network policies instate rules to control the network traffic either from or to a Pod. You can think of network policies as firewall rules for Pods. It's best practice to start with a "deny all traffic" rule to minimize the attack vector. From there, you can open access as needed. Learning about the intricacies of network policies requires a bit of hands-on practice, as it is not directly apparent if the rules work as expected.

Exam Essentials

Understand the purpose of a Service

The key takeaway for wanting to create a Service is that Pods expose an IP address but virtual and dyanmic IP address can't be relied upon. The IP address automatically changes whenever the Pod needs to be restarted—for example, as a result of a liveness probe identifying that the application doesn't work properly or a node drain/failure event. A Service creates a unified network interface and can expose a set of Pods associated with a label selector.

Practice the implications of different Service types

Reading about the theoretical effect of assigning specific Service types won't be sufficient to prepare for the CKAD exam. You will need to practically experience their impact by making Pods accessible from within or outside of the cluster. Spend extra time on the differences between `ClusterIP` and `NodePort`.

Know the basics about network policies

The CKAD curriculum doesn't clearly state the depth of knowledge you need to have about network policies. I'd recommend going deeper than you would expect for the exam. Network policies come with a couple of basic rules. Once you understand those, it should be relatively easy to grasp their influence on accessibility. To explore common scenarios, have a look at the GitHub repository named "Kubernetes Network Policy Recipes" (*https://oreil.ly/1ARKk*). The repository comes with a visual representation for each scenario and walks you through the steps to set up the network policy and the involed Pods. This is a great practicing resource.

Sample Exercises

Solutions to these exercises are available in the Appendix.

1. Create a new Pod named `frontend` that uses the image `nginx`. Assign the labels `tier=frontend` and `app=nginx`. Expose the container port 80.

2. Create a new Pod named `backend` that uses the image `nginx`. Assign the labels `tier=backend` and `app=nginx`. Expose the container port 80.

3. Create a new Service named `nginx-service` of type `ClusterIP`. Assign the port 9000 and the target port 80. The label selector should use the criteria `tier=back end` and `deployment=app`.

4. Try to access the set of Pods through the Service from within the cluster. Which Pods does the Service select?

5. Fix the Service assignment to properly select the `backend` Pod and assign the correct target port.

6. Expose the Service to be accessible from outside of the cluster. Make a call to the Service.

7. Assume an application stack that defines three different layers: a frontend, a backend, and a database. Each of the layers runs in a Pod. You can find the definition in the YAML file *app-stack.yaml*:

```
kind: Pod
apiVersion: v1
metadata:
  name: frontend
  namespace: app-stack
  labels:
    app: todo
    tier: frontend
```

```
spec:
  containers:
  - name: frontend
    image: nginx

---

kind: Pod
apiVersion: v1
metadata:
  name: backend
  namespace: app-stack
  labels:
    app: todo
    tier: backend
spec:
  containers:
  - name: backend
    image: nginx

---

kind: Pod
apiVersion: v1
metadata:
  name: database
  namespace: app-stack
  labels:
    app: todo
    tier: database
spec:
  containers:
  - name: database
    image: mysql
    env:
    - name: MYSQL_ROOT_PASSWORD
      value: example
```

Create the namespace and the Pods using the file *app-stack.yaml*.

8. Create a network policy in the file *app-stack-network-policy.yaml*. The network policy should allow incoming traffic from the backend to the database but disallow incoming traffic from the frontend.

9. Reconfigure the network policy to only allow incoming traffic to the database on TCP port 3306 and no other port.

## CHAPTER 8

State Persistence

Each container running in a Pod provides a temporary filesystem. Applications running in the container can read from it and write to it. A container's temporary filesystem is isolated from any other container or Pod and is not persisted beyond a Pod restart. The "State Persistence" section of the CKAD curriculum addresses the technical abstraction in Kubernetes responsible for persisting data beyond a container or Pod restart.

A Volume is a Kubernetes capability that persists data beyond a Pod restart. Essentially, a Volume is a directory that's shareable between multiple containers of a Pod. You will learn about the different Volume types and the process for defining and mounting a Volume in a container.

Persistent Volumes are a specific category of the wider concept of Volumes. The mechanics for Persistent Volumes are slightly more complex. The Persistent Volume is the resource that actually persists the data to an underlying physical storage. The Persistent Volume Claim represents the connecting resource between a Pod and a Persistent Volume responsible for requesting the storage. Finally, the Pod needs to *claim* the Persistent Volume and mount it to a directory path available to the containers running inside of the Pod.

At a high level, this chapter covers the following concepts:

- Volume
- Persistent Volume
- Persistent Volume Claim

Understanding Volumes

Applications running in a container can use the temporary filesystem to read and write files. In case of a container crash or a cluster/node restart, the kubelet will restart the container. Any data that had been written to the temporary filesystem is lost and cannot be retrieved anymore. The container effectively starts with a clean slate again.

There are many uses cases for wanting to mount a Volume in a container. We already saw one of the most prominent use cases in Chapter 4 that uses a Volume to exchange data between a main application container and a sidecar. Figure 8-1 illustrates the differences between the temporary filesystem of a container and the use of a Volume.

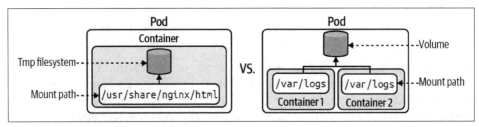

Figure 8-1. A container using the temporary filesystem versus a Volume

Volume Types

Every Volume needs to define a type. The type determines the medium that backs the Volume and its runtime behavior. The Kubernetes documentation offers a long list of Volume types. Some of the types—for example, `azureDisk`, `awsElasticBlockStore`, or `gcePersistentDisk`—are only available when running the Kubernetes cluster in a specific cloud provider. Table 8-1 shows a reduced list of Volume types that I deem to be most relevant to the CKAD exam.

Table 8-1. Volume types relevant to CKAD exam

Type	Description
emptyDir	Empty directory in Pod with read/write access. Only persisted for the lifespan of a Pod. A good choice for cache implementations or data exchange between containers of a Pod.
hostPath	File or directory from the host node's filesystem.
configMap, secret	Provides a way to inject configuration data. For practical examples, see Chapter 3.
nfs	An existing NFS (Network File System) share. Preserves data after Pod restart.
persistentVolumeClaim	Claims a Persistent Volume. Fore more information, see "Creating PersistentVolumeClaims" on page 134.

Creating and Accessing Volumes

Defining a Volume for a Pod requires two steps. First, you need to declare the Volume itself using the attribute `spec.volumes`. As part of the definition, you provide the name and the type. Just declaring the Volume won't be sufficient, though. Second, the Volume needs to be mounted to a path of the consuming container via `spec.containers.volumeMounts`. The mapping between the Volume and the Volume mount occurs by the matching name.

In Example 8-1, stored in the file *pod-with-volume.yaml* here, you can see the definition of a Volume with type `emptyDir`. The Volume has been mounted to the path */var/logs* inside of the container named `nginx`:

Example 8-1. A Pod defining and mounting a Volume

```
apiVersion: v1
kind: Pod
metadata:
  name: business-app
spec:
  volumes:
  - name: logs-volume
    emptyDir: {}
  containers:
  - image: nginx
    name: nginx
    volumeMounts:
    - mountPath: /var/logs
      name: logs-volume
```

Let's create the Pod and see if we can interact with the mounted Volume. The following commands open an interactive shell after the Pod's creation, then navigate to the mount path. You can see that the Volume type `emptyDir` initializes the mount path as an empty directory. New files and directories can be created as needed without limitations:

```
$ kubectl create -f pod-with-volume.yaml
pod/business-app created
$ kubectl get pod business-app
NAME            READY    STATUS     RESTARTS    AGE
business-app    1/1      Running    0           43s
$ kubectl exec business-app -it -- /bin/sh
# cd /var/logs
# pwd
/var/logs
# ls
# touch app-logs.txt
# ls
app-logs.txt
```

For an illustrative use case of the `emptyDir` Volume type mounted by more than one container, see Chapter 4.

Understanding Persistent Volumes

Data stored on Volumes outlive a container restart. In many applications, the data lives far beyond the lifecycles of the applications, container, Pod, nodes, and even the clusters themselves. Data persistence ensures the lifecycles of the data are decoupled from the lifecycles of the cluster resources. A typical example would be data persisted by a database. That's the responsibility of a Persistent Volume. Kubernetes models persist data with the help of two primitives: the PersistentVolume and the Persistent-VolumeClaim.

The PersistentVolume is the storage device in a Kubernetes cluster. The PersistentVo-lume is completely decoupled from the Pod and therefore has its own lifecycle. The object captures the source of the storage (e.g., storage made available by a cloud pro-vider). A PersistentVolume is either provided by a Kubernetes administrator or assigned dynamically by mapping to a storage class.

The PersistentVolumeClaim requests the resources of a PersistentVolume—for example, the size of the storage and the access type. In the Pod, you will use the type `persistentVolumeClaim` to mount the abstracted PersistentVolume by using the PersistentVolumeClaim.

Figure 8-2 shows the relationship between the Pod, the PersistentVolumeClaim, and the PersistentVolume.

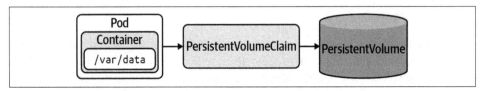

Figure 8-2. Claiming a PersistentVolume from a Pod

Static Versus Dynamic Provisioning

A PersistentVolume can be created statically or dynamically. If you go with the static approach, then you need to create storage device first and reference it by explicitly creating an object of kind PersistentVolume. The dynamic approach doesn't require you to create a PersistentVolume object. It will be automatically created from the PersistentVolumeClaim by setting a storage class name using the attribute `spec.storageClassName`.

A storage class is an abstraction concept that defines a class of storage device (e.g., storage with slow or fast performance) used for different application types. It's usually the job of a Kubernetes administrator to set up storage classes. Minikube already creates a default storage class named `standard`, which you can query with the following command:

```
$ kubectl get storageclass
NAME                PROVISIONER             RECLAIMPOLICY   VOLUMEBINDINGMODE \
  ALLOWVOLUMEEXPANSION   AGE
standard (default)  k8s.io/minikube-hostpath  Delete        Immediate \
  false               108d
```

A deeper discussion on storage classes (*https://oreil.ly/SdFJB*) is out of scope for this book. For the CKAD exam, you will only need to understand the purpose of a storage class, how to set it, and its dynamic creation behavior of a PersistentVolume.

Creating PersistentVolumes

A PersistentVolume can only be created using the mainfest-first approach. At this time, `kubectl` does not allow the creation of a PersistentVolume using the `create` command. Every PersistentVolume needs to define the storage capacity using `spec.capacity` and an access mode set via `spec.accessModes`. Table 8-2 provides a high-level overview of the available access modes.

Table 8-2. PersistentVolume access modes

Type	Description
ReadWriteOnce	Read/write access by a single node.
ReadOnlyMany	Read-only access by many nodes.
ReadWriteMany	Read/write access by many nodes.

Example 8-2 creates a PersistentVolume named db-pv with a storage capacity of 1Gi and read/write access by a single node. The attribute `hostPath` mounts the directory */data/db* from the host node's filesystem. We'll store the YAML mainfest in the file *db-pv.yaml*.

Example 8-2. YAML manifest defining a PersistentVolume

```
apiVersion: v1
kind: PersistentVolume
metadata:
  name: db-pv
spec:
  capacity:
    storage: 1Gi
  accessModes:
    - ReadWriteOnce
```

```
  hostPath:
    path: /data/db
```

Upon inspection of the created PersistentVolume, you'll find most of the information you provided in the manifest. The status `Available` indicates that the object is ready to be claimed. The reclaim policy determines what should happen with the PersistentVolume after it has been released from its claim. By default, the object will be retained. The following example uses the short-form command pv to avoid having to type `persistentvolume`:

```
$ kubectl create -f db-pv.yaml
persistentvolume/db-pv created
$ kubectl get pv db-pv
NAME    CAPACITY   ACCESS MODES   RECLAIM POLICY   STATUS      CLAIM    STORAGECLASS \
   REASON   AGE
db-pv   1Gi        RWO            Retain           Available \
           10s
```

Creating PersistentVolumeClaims

The next object we'll need to create is the PersistentVolumeClaim. Its purpose is to bind the PersistentVolume to the Pod. Let's have a look at the YAML manifest stored in the file *db-pvc.yaml*, as shown in Example 8-3.

Example 8-3. Definition of a PersistentVolumeClaim

```
kind: PersistentVolumeClaim
apiVersion: v1
metadata:
  name: db-pvc
spec:
  accessModes:
    - ReadWriteOnce
  resources:
    requests:
      storage: 512m
```

What we're saying here is, "Give me a PersistentVolume that can fulfill the resource request of 512m and provides the access mode `ReadWriteOnce`." The binding to an appropriate PersistentVolume happens automatically based on those criteria.

After creating the PersistentVolumeClaim, the status is set as `Bound`, which means that the binding to the PersistentVolume was successful. The following get command uses the short-form pvc instead of `persistentvolumeclaims`:

```
$ kubectl create -f db-pvc.yaml
persistentvolumeclaim/db-pvc created
$ kubectl get pvc db-pvc
```

```
NAME     STATUS  VOLUME                                      CAPACITY  ACCESS MODES \
  STORAGECLASS   AGE
db-pvc   Bound   pvc-c9e9aa9e-890d-4fd1-96e6-64072366f78d   512m       RWO \
  standard       7s
```

The PersistentVolume has not been mounted by a Pod yet. Therefore, inspecting the details of the object shows <none>. Using the describe command is a good way to verify if the PersistentVolumeClaim was mounted properly:

```
$ kubectl describe pvc db-pvc
...
Mounted By:     <none>
...
```

Mounting PersistentVolumeClaims in a Pod

All that's left is mounting the PersistentVolumeClaim in the Pod that wants to consume it. You already learned how to mount a Volume in a Pod. The big difference here, shown in Example 8-4, is using spec.volumes.persistentVolumeClaim and providing the name of the PersistentVolumeClaim.

Example 8-4. A Pod referencing a PersistentVolumeClaim

```
apiVersion: v1
kind: Pod
metadata:
  name: app-consuming-pvc
spec:
  volumes:
    - name: app-storage
      persistentVolumeClaim:
        claimName: db-pvc
  containers:
  - image: alpine
    name: app
    command: ["/bin/sh"]
    args: ["-c", "while true; do sleep 60; done;"]
    volumeMounts:
      - mountPath: "/mnt/data"
        name: app-storage
```

Let's assume we stored the configuration in the file *app-consuming-pvc.yaml*. After creating the Pod from the manifest, you should see the Pod transitioning into the Ready state. The describe command will provide additional information on the Volume:

```
$ kubectl create -f app-consuming-pvc.yaml
pod/app-consuming-pvc created
$ kubectl get pods
```

```
NAME                  READY   STATUS    RESTARTS   AGE
app-consuming-pvc     1/1     Running   0          3s
$ kubectl describe pod app-consuming-pvc
...
Volumes:
  app-storage:
    Type:       PersistentVolumeClaim (a reference to a PersistentVolumeClaim \
                in the same namespace)
    ClaimName:  db-pvc
    ReadOnly:   false
...
```

The PersistentVolumeClaim now also shows the Pod that mounted it:

```
$ kubectl describe pvc db-pvc
...
Mounted By:    app-consuming-pvc
...
```

You can now go ahead and open an interactive shell to the Pod. Navigating to the mount path at */mnt/data* gives you access to the underlying PersistentVolume:

```
$ kubectl exec app-consuming-pvc -it -- /bin/sh
/ # cd /mnt/data
/mnt/data # ls -l
total 0
/mnt/data # touch test.db
/mnt/data # ls -l
total 0
-rw-r--r--    1 root     root             0 Sep 29 23:59 test.db
```

Summary

Containers store data in a temporary filesystem, which is empty each time a new Pod is started. Application developers need to persist data beyond the lifecycles of the containers, Pods, node, and cluster. Typical examples include persistent log files or data in a database.

Kubernetes offers the concept of a Volume to implement the use case. A Pod mounts a Volume to a path in the container. Any data written to the mounted storage will be persisted beyond a container restart. Kubernetes offers a wide range of Volume types to fulfill different requirements.

PersistentVolumes even store data beyond a Pod or cluster/node restart. Those objects are decoupled from the Pod's lifecycle and are therefore represented by a Kubernetes primitive. The PersistentVolumeClaim abstracts the underlying implementation details of a PersistentVolume and acts as an intermediary between Pod and PersistentVolume.

Exam Essentials

Understand the need and use cases for a Volume

Many production-ready application stacks running in a cloud native environment need to persist data. Read up on common use cases and explore recipes that describe typical scenarios. You can find some examples in the O'Reilly books *Kubernetes Patterns* (*https://oreil.ly/mQKRj*), *Kubernetes Best Practices* (*https://oreil.ly/hcFNA*), and *Cloud Native DevOps with Kubernetes* (*https://oreil.ly/G7V3W*).

Practice defining and consuming Volumes

Volumes are a cross-cutting concept applied in different areas of the CKAD exam. Know where to find the relevant documentation for defining a Volume and the multitude of ways to consume a Volume from a container. Definitely revisit Chapter 3 for a deep dive on how to mount ConfigMaps and Secrets as a Volume, and Chapter 4 for coverage on sharing a Volume between two containers.

Internalize the mechanics of defining and consuming a PersistentVolume

Creating a PersistentVolume involves a couple of moving parts. Understand the configuration options for PeristentVolumes and PersistentVolumeClaims and how they play together. Try to emulate situations that prevent a successful binding of a PersistentVolumeClaim. Then fix the situation by taking counteractions. Internalize the short-form commands pv and pvc to save precious time during the exam.

Sample Exercises

Solutions to these exercises are available in the Appendix.

1. Create a Pod YAML file with two containers that use the image alpine:3.12.0. Provide a command for both containers that keep them running forever.

2. Define a Volume of type emptyDir for the Pod. Container 1 should mount the Volume to path */etc/a*, and container 2 should mount the Volume to path */etc/b*.

3. Open an interactive shell for container 1 and create the directory *data* in the mount path. Navigate to the directory and create the file *hello.txt* with the contents "Hello World." Exit out of the container.

4. Open an interactive shell for container 2 and navigate to the directory */etc/b/ data*. Inspect the contents of file *hello.txt*. Exit out of the container.

5. Create a PersistentVolume named logs-pv that maps to the hostPath */var/logs*. The access mode should be ReadWriteOnce and ReadOnlyMany. Provision a

storage capacity of 5Gi. Ensure that the status of the PersistentVolume shows `Available`.

6. Create a PersistentVolumeClaim named `logs-pvc`. The access it uses is `ReadWriteOnce`. Request a capacity of 2Gi. Ensure that the status of the PersistentVolume shows `Bound`.

7. Mount the PersistentVolumeClaim in a Pod running the image `nginx` at the mount path */var/log/nginx*.

8. Open an interactive shell to the container and create a new file named *my-nginx.log* in */var/log/nginx*. Exit out of the Pod.

9. Delete the Pod and re-create it with the same YAML manifest. Open an interactive shell to the Pod, navigate to the directory */var/log/nginx*, and find the file you created before.

Answers to Review Questions

Chapter 2, Core Concepts

1. You can either use the imperative approach or the declarative approach. First, we'll look at creating the namespace with the imperative approach:

   ```
   $ kubectl create namespace ckad
   ```

   Create the Pod:

   ```
   $ kubectl run nginx --image=nginx:1.17.10 --port=80 --namespace=ckad
   ```

   Alternatively, you can use the declarative approach. Create a new YAML file called *ckad-namespace.yaml* with the following contents:

   ```
   apiVersion: v1
   kind: Namespace
   metadata:
     name: ckad
   ```

   Create the namespace from the YAML file:

   ```
   $ kubectl create -f ckad-namespace.yaml
   ```

   Create a new YAML file called *nginx-pod.yaml* with the following contents:

   ```
   apiVersion: v1
   kind: Pod
   metadata:
     name: nginx
   spec:
     containers:
     - name: nginx
       image: nginx:1.17.10
       ports:
       - containerPort: 80
   ```

Create the Pod from the YAML file:

```
$ kubectl create -f nginx-pod.yaml --namespace=ckad
```

2. You can use the command-line option -o wide to retrieve the IP address of the Pod:

```
$ kubectl get pod nginx --namespace=ckad -o wide
```

The same information is available if you query for the Pod details:

```
$ kubectl describe pod nginx --namespace=ckad | grep IP:
```

3. You can use the command-line options --rm and -it to start a temporary Pod. The following command assumes that the IP address of the Pod named nginx is 10.1.0.66:

```
$ kubectl run busybox --image=busybox --restart=Never --rm -it -n ckad \
  -- wget -O- 10.1.0.66:80
```

4. To download the logs, use a simple logs command:

```
$ kubectl logs nginx --namespace=ckad
```

5. Editing the live object is forbidden. You will receive an error message if you try to add the environment variables:

```
$ kubectl edit pod nginx --namespace=ckad
```

You will have to re-create the object with a modified YAML file, but first you'll have to delete the existing object:

```
$ kubectl delete pod nginx --namespace=ckad
```

Edit the existing YAML file *nginx-pod.yaml*:

```
apiVersion: v1
kind: Pod
metadata:
  name: nginx
spec:
  containers:
  - name: nginx
    image: nginx:1.17.10
    ports:
    - containerPort: 80
    env:
    - name: DB_URL
      value: postgresql://mydb:5432
    - name: DB_USERNAME
      value: admin
```

Apply the changes:

```
$ kubectl create -f nginx-pod.yaml --namespace=ckad
```

6. Use the exec command to open an interactive shell to the container:

```
$ kubectl exec -it nginx --namespace=ckad  -- /bin/sh
# ls -l
```

7. Combine the command-line options `-o yaml` and `--dry-run=client` to write the generated YAML to a file. Make sure to escape the double-quote characters of the string rendered by the echo command:

```
$ kubectl run loop --image=busybox -o yaml --dry-run=client \
  --restart=Never -- /bin/sh -c 'for i in 1 2 3 4 5 6 7 8 9 10; \
  do echo "Welcome $i times"; done' \
  > pod.yaml
```

Create the Pod from the YAML file:

```
$ kubectl create -f pod.yaml --namespace=ckad
```

The status of the Pod will say `Completed`, as the executed command in the container does not run in an infinite loop:

```
$ kubectl get pod loop --namespace=ckad
```

8. The container command cannot be changed for existing Pods. Delete the Pod so you can modify the manifest file and re-create the object:

```
$ kubectl delete pod loop --namespace=ckad
```

Change the YAML file content:

```
apiVersion: v1
kind: Pod
metadata:
  creationTimestamp: null
  labels:
    run: loop
  name: loop
spec:
  containers:
  - args:
    - /bin/sh
    - -c
    - while true; do date; sleep 10; done
    image: busybox
    name: loop
    resources: {}
  dnsPolicy: ClusterFirst
  restartPolicy: Never
status: {}
```

Create the Pod from the YAML file:

```
$ kubectl create -f pod.yaml --namespace=ckad
```

9. You can describe the Pod events by grepping for the term:

```
$ kubectl describe pod loop --namespace=ckad | grep -C 10 Events:
```

10. You can simply delete the namespace, which will delete all objects within the namespace:

```
$ kubectl delete namespace ckad
```

Chapter 3, Configuration

1. The easiest way to create a Secret is with the help of the imperative approach, as you do not have to Base64-encode the values manually. Start by creating the directory and relevant files. The following commands achieve this for Unix, Linux, and macOS platforms. Of course, you can also create the files and content by hand with the help of an editor:

```
$ mkdir config
$ echo -e "password=mypwd" > config/db.txt
$ echo -e "api_key=LmLHbYhsgWZwNifiqaRorH8T" > config/ext-service.txt
$ ls config
db.txt          ext-service.txt
```

2. Use the imperative approach to create a new Secret by pointing it to the *config* directory. Upon inspection of the live object, you will find each key uses the name of the configuration file. The values have been Base64-encoded:

```
$ kubectl create secret generic ext-service-secret --from-file=config
secret/ext-service-secret created
$ kubectl get secret ext-service-secret -o yaml
apiVersion: v1
data:
  db.txt: cGFzc3dvcmQ9bXlwd2QK
  ext-service.txt: YXBpX2tleT1MbUxIYlloc2dXWndOaWZpcWFSb3JIOFQK
kind: Secret
metadata:
  creationTimestamp: "2020-07-12T23:56:33Z"
  managedFields:
  - apiVersion: v1
    fieldsType: FieldsV1
    fieldsV1:
      f:data:
        .: {}
        f:db.txt: {}
        f:ext-service.txt: {}
      f:type: {}
    manager: kubectl
    operation: Update
    time: "2020-07-12T23:56:33Z"
  name: ext-service-secret
  namespace: default
  resourceVersion: "1462456"
```

```
selfLink: /api/v1/namespaces/default/secrets/ext-service-secret
uid: b7f4faae-e624-4027-8bcf-af385019a8d8
type: Opaque
```

3. As a starting point, generate the YAML manifest of the Pod.

```
$ kubectl run consumer --image=nginx --dry-run=client --restart=Never \
-o yaml > pod.yaml
```

Next, modify the manifest by mounting the Secret as a Volume. The end result could look like the following YAML definition:

```
apiVersion: v1
kind: Pod
metadata:
  creationTimestamp: null
  labels:
    run: consumer
  name: consumer
spec:
  containers:
  - image: nginx
    name: consumer
    volumeMounts:
    - name: secret-volume
      mountPath: /var/app
      readOnly: true
    resources: {}
  volumes:
  - name: secret-volume
    secret:
      secretName: ext-service-secret
  dnsPolicy: ClusterFirst
  restartPolicy: Never
status: {}
```

Now, create the Pod. Shell into the Pod as soon as the status indicates Running. Navigate to the directory */var/app*. Each key-value pair of the Secret exists as a file and observes its plain-text value as content:

```
$ kubectl create -f pod.yaml
pod/consumer created
$ kubectl get pod consumer
NAME       READY   STATUS    RESTARTS   AGE
consumer   1/1     Running   0          17s
$ kubectl exec consumer -it -- /bin/sh
# cd /var/app
# ls
db.txt  ext-service.txt
# cat db.txt
password=mypwd
# cat ext-service.txt
```

```
api_key=LmLHbYhsgWZwNifiqaRorH8T
# exit
```

4. It's usually easier and faster to create a ConfigMap by running an imperative command. Here, we'll want to practice the declarative approach. A YAML manifest for a ConfigMap with the expected key-value pairs could look as follows:

```
apiVersion: v1
kind: ConfigMap
metadata:
  name: ext-service-configmap
data:
  api_endpoint: https://myapp.com/api
  username: bot
```

With this definition, create the object:

```
$ kubectl create -f configmap.yaml
configmap/ext-service-configmap created
$ kubectl get configmap ext-service-configmap
NAME                    DATA   AGE
ext-service-configmap   2      36s
$ kubectl get configmap ext-service-configmap -o yaml
apiVersion: v1
data:
  api_endpoint: https://myapp.com/api
  username: bot
kind: ConfigMap
metadata:
  creationTimestamp: "2020-07-13T00:17:43Z"
  managedFields:
  - apiVersion: v1
    fieldsType: FieldsV1
    fieldsV1:
      f:data:
        .: {}
        f:api_endpoint: {}
        f:username: {}
    manager: kubectl
    operation: Update
    time: "2020-07-13T00:17:43Z"
  name: ext-service-configmap
  namespace: default
  resourceVersion: "1465228"
  selfLink: /api/v1/namespaces/default/configmaps/ext-service-configmap
  uid: b1b51b17-2dad-4320-b7c2-6758feca3800
```

5. The keys of the ConfigMap configuration data do not follow typical naming conventions of environment variables. Without modifying the keys in the Config-Map, you can still map them to a more reasonable naming convention when injecting them into the Pod. You will have to re-create the Pod to make the

---

necessary changes as Kubernetes doesn't allow adding new environment variables to a running container. The resulting YAML manifest could look like the following code snippet:

```yaml
apiVersion: v1
kind: Pod
metadata:
  creationTimestamp: null
  labels:
    run: consumer
  name: consumer
spec:
  containers:
  - image: nginx
    name: consumer
    volumeMounts:
    - name: secret-volume
      mountPath: /var/app
      readOnly: true
    env:
    - name: API_ENDPOINT
      valueFrom:
        configMapKeyRef:
          name: ext-service-configmap
          key: api_endpoint
    - name: USERNAME
      valueFrom:
        configMapKeyRef:
          name: ext-service-configmap
          key: username
  volumes:
  - name: secret-volume
    secret:
      secretName: ext-service-secret
  dnsPolicy: ClusterFirst
  restartPolicy: Always
status: {}
```

6. You should be able to find the environment variable with the proper name by running the env command from within the container:

```
$ kubectl exec -it consumer -- /bin/sh
# env
...
API_ENDPOINT=https://myapp.com/api
USERNAME=bot
...
# exit
```

7. You can get started by creating the Pod manifest using the run command:

```
$ kubectl run security-context-demo --image=alpine --dry-run=client \
   --restart=Never -o yaml > pod.yaml
```

Edit the file *pod.yaml* and add the security context. The Linux capability cannot be overridden at the Pod level for two reasons. On the one hand, Linux capabilities can only be defined at the container level. On the other hand, a Pod-level definition does not redefine the container-level security context—it's the other way around:

```
apiVersion: v1
kind: Pod
metadata:
  creationTimestamp: null
  labels:
    run: security-context-demo
  name: security-context-demo
spec:
  containers:
  - image: alpine
    name: security-context-demo
    resources: {}
    securityContext:
      capabilities:
        add: ["SYS_TIME"]
  dnsPolicy: ClusterFirst
  restartPolicy: Never
status: {}
```

8. Start by creating the new namespace:

```
$ kubectl create namespace project-firebird
namespace/project-firebird created
$ kubectl get namespace project-firebird
NAME              STATUS   AGE
project-firebird  Active   23s
```

Create a YAML manifest for the ResourceQuota. You can define the maximum count of Secrets in the namespace with the attribute `spec.hard.secrets`:

```
apiVersion: v1
kind: ResourceQuota
metadata:
  name: firebird-quota
spec:
  hard:
    secrets: 1
```

Say you stored the manifest in the file *resource-quota.yaml*; you can create it with the following command. Make sure to provide the namespace:

```
$ kubectl create -f resource-quota.yaml --namespace=project-firebird
resourcequota/firebird-quota created
```

9. You will notice that the namespace already contains a Secret that belongs to the default Service Account. Effectively, your maximum count of Secrets has already been reached:

```
$ kubectl get resourcequota firebird-quota --namespace=project-firebird
NAME            AGE   REQUEST        LIMIT
firebird-quota  39s   secrets: 1/1
$ kubectl get secrets --namespace=project-firebird
NAME                TYPE                                  DATA  AGE
default-token-mdcd8  kubernetes.io/service-account-token   3     7m54s
```

Now, go ahead and create a Secret. The ResourceQuota will render an error message and disallow the creation of the Secret:

```
$ kubectl create secret generic my-secret --from-literal=test=hello \
  --namespace=project-firebird
Error from server (Forbidden): secrets "my-secret" is forbidden: \
exceeded quota: firebird-quota, requested: secrets=1, used: secrets=1, \
limited: secrets=1
```

10. You can go through the whole process by running imperative commands. Start by creating the custom Service Account, then create a new Pod and use the command-line option `--serviceaccount` to assign the Service Account. You can find the authentication token in the container's directory */var/run/secrets/kubernetes.io/serviceaccount/token*:

```
$ kubectl create serviceaccount monitoring
serviceaccount/monitoring created
$ kubectl get serviceaccount monitoring
NAME        SECRETS  AGE
monitoring  1        12s
$ kubectl run nginx --image=nginx --restart=Never \
  --serviceaccount=monitoring
pod/nginx created
$ kubectl exec -it nginx -- /bin/sh
# cat /var/run/secrets/kubernetes.io/serviceaccount/token
eyJhbGci0...rH4fkeYsw
```

Chapter 4, Multi-Container Pods

1. You can start by generating the YAML manifest in dry-run mode. The resulting manifest will set up the main application container:

```
$ kubectl run complex-pod --image=nginx --port=80 --restart=Never \
  -o yaml --dry-run=client > complex-pod.yaml
```

Edit the manifest file by adding the init container and changing some of the default settings that have been generated. The finalized manifest could look as follows:

```
apiVersion: v1
kind: Pod
metadata:
  name: complex-pod
spec:
  initContainers:
  - image: busybox
    name: setup
    command: ['sh', '-c', 'wget -O- google.com']
  containers:
  - image: nginx
    name: app
    ports:
    - containerPort: 80
    resources: {}
  dnsPolicy: ClusterFirst
  restartPolicy: Never
status: {}
```

2. Run the `create` command to instantiate the Pod. Verify that the Pod is running without issues:

```
$ kubectl create -f complex-pod.yaml
pod/complex-pod created
$ kubectl get pod complex-pod
NAME          READY    STATUS     RESTARTS    AGE
complex-pod   1/1      Running    0           27s
```

3. Use the `logs` command and point it to the init container to download the log output:

```
$ kubectl logs complex-pod -c setup
Connecting to google.com (172.217.1.206:80)
Connecting to www.google.com (172.217.2.4:80)
writing to stdout
...
```

4. You can target the main application as well. Here you'll open an interactive shell and run the `ls` command:

```
$ kubectl exec complex-pod -it -c app -- /bin/sh
# ls
bin  dev  docker-entrypoint.sh  home  lib64  mnt  proc  run \
srv  tmp  var  boot  docker-entrypoint.d  etclib  media  opt \
root  sbin  sys  usr
# exit
```

5. Avoid graceful deletion of the Pod by adding the options `--grace-period=0` and `--force`:

```
$ kubectl delete pod complex-pod --grace-period=0 --force
warning: Immediate deletion does not wait for confirmation that the \
```

running resource has been terminated. The resource may continue to run \
on the cluster indefinitely.
pod "complex-pod" force deleted

6. You can start by generating the YAML manifest in dry-run mode. The resulting manifest will set up the main application container:

```
$ kubectl run data-exchange --image=busybox --restart=Never -o yaml \
  --dry-run=client > data-exchange.yaml
```

Edit the manifest file by adding the sidecar container and changing some of the default settings that have been generated. The finalized manifest could look as follows:

```
apiVersion: v1
kind: Pod
metadata:
  name: data-exchange
spec:
  containers:
  - image: busybox
    name: main-app
    command: ['sh', '-c', 'counter=1; while true; do touch \
              "/var/app/data/$counter-data.txt"; counter=$((counter+1)); \
              sleep 30; done']
    resources: {}
  dnsPolicy: ClusterFirst
  restartPolicy: Never
status: {}
```

7. Simply add the sidecar container alongside the main application container with the proper command. Add on to the existing YAML manifest:

```
apiVersion: v1
kind: Pod
metadata:
  name: data-exchange
spec:
  containers:
  - image: busybox
    name: main-app
    command: ['sh', '-c', 'counter=1; while true; do touch \
              "/var/app/data/$counter-data.txt"; counter=$((counter+1)); \
              sleep 30; done']
    resources: {}
  - image: busybox
    name: sidecar
    command: ['sh', '-c', 'while true; do ls -dq /var/app/data/*-data.txt \
              | wc -l; sleep 30; done']
  dnsPolicy: ClusterFirst
  restartPolicy: Never
status: {}
```

8. Modify the manifest so that a Volume is used to exchange the files between the main application container and sidecar container:

```yaml
apiVersion: v1
kind: Pod
metadata:
  name: data-exchange
spec:
  containers:
  - image: busybox
    name: main-app
    command: ['sh', '-c', 'counter=1; while true; do touch \
                "/var/app/data/$counter-data.txt"; counter=$((counter+1)); \
                sleep 30; done']
    volumeMounts:
    - name: data-dir
      mountPath: "/var/app/data"
    resources: {}
  - image: busybox
    name: sidecar
    command: ['sh', '-c', 'while true; do ls -d /var/app/data/*-data.txt \
                | wc -l; sleep 30; done']
    volumeMounts:
    - name: data-dir
      mountPath: "/var/app/data"
  volumes:
  - name: data-dir
    emptyDir: {}
  dnsPolicy: ClusterFirst
  restartPolicy: Never
status: {}
```

9. Create the Pod, check for its existence, and tail the logs of the sidecar container. The number of files will increment over time:

```
$ kubectl create -f data-exchange.yaml
pod/data-exchange created
$ kubectl get pod data-exchange
NAME            READY   STATUS    RESTARTS   AGE
data-exchange   2/2     Running   0          31s
$ kubectl logs data-exchange -c sidecar -f
1
2
...
```

10. Delete the Pod:

```
$ kubectl delete pod data-exchange
pod "data-exchange" deleted
```

Chapter 5, Observability

1. You can start by generating the YAML manifest in dry-run mode. The resulting manifest will create the container with the proper image:

   ```
   $ kubectl run web-server --image=nginx --port=80 --restart=Never \
     -o yaml --dry-run=client > probed-pod.yaml
   ```

2. Edit the manifest by defining a startup probe. The finalized manifest could look as follows:

   ```
   apiVersion: v1
   kind: Pod
   metadata:
     creationTimestamp: null
     labels:
       run: web-server
     name: web-server
   spec:
     containers:
     - image: nginx
       name: web-server
       ports:
       - containerPort: 80
         name: nginx-port
       startupProbe:
         httpGet:
           path: /
           port: nginx-port
       resources: {}
     dnsPolicy: ClusterFirst
     restartPolicy: Never
   status: {}
   ```

3. Further edit the manifest by defining a readiness probe. The finalized manifest could look as follows:

   ```
   apiVersion: v1
   kind: Pod
   metadata:
     creationTimestamp: null
     labels:
       run: web-server
     name: web-server
   spec:
     containers:
     - image: nginx
       name: web-server
       ports:
       - containerPort: 80
         name: nginx-port
   ```

```
      startupProbe:
        httpGet:
          path: /
          port: nginx-port
      readinessProbe:
        httpGet:
          path: /
          port: nginx-port
          initialDelaySeconds: 5
      resources: {}
    dnsPolicy: ClusterFirst
    restartPolicy: Never
  status: {}
```

4. Further edit the manifest by defining a liveness probe. The finalized manifest could look as follows:

```
apiVersion: v1
kind: Pod
metadata:
  creationTimestamp: null
  labels:
    run: web-server
  name: web-server
spec:
  containers:
  - image: nginx
    name: web-server
    ports:
    - containerPort: 80
      name: nginx-port
    startupProbe:
      httpGet:
        path: /
        port: nginx-port
    readinessProbe:
      httpGet:
        path: /
        port: nginx-port
      initialDelaySeconds: 5
    livenessProbe:
      httpGet:
        path: /
        port: nginx-port
      initialDelaySeconds: 10
      periodSeconds: 30
    resources: {}
  dnsPolicy: ClusterFirst
  restartPolicy: Never
status: {}
```

5. Create the Pod, then check its READY and STATUS columns. The container will transition from ContainerCreating to Running. At some point, 1/1 container will be available:

```
$ kubectl create -f probed-pod.yaml
pod/probed-pod created
$ kubectl get pod web-server
NAME          READY    STATUS             RESTARTS   AGE
web-server    0/1      ContainerCreating  0          7s
$ kubectl get pod web-server
NAME          READY    STATUS     RESTARTS   AGE
web-server    0/1      Running    0          8s
$ kubectl get pod web-server
NAME          READY    STATUS     RESTARTS   AGE
web-server    1/1      Running    0          38s
```

6. You should find the configuration of the probes when executing the describe command:

```
$ kubectl describe pod web-server
...
Containers:
  web-server:
    ...
    Ready:          True
    Restart Count:  0
    Liveness:       http-get http://:nginx-port/ delay=10s timeout=1s \
                    period=30s #success=1 #failure=3
    Readiness:      http-get http://:nginx-port/ delay=5s timeout=1s \
                    period=10s #success=1 #failure=3
    Startup:        http-get http://:nginx-port/ delay=0s timeout=1s \
                    period=10s #success=1 #failure=3
    ...
```

7. Run the top command to retrieve monitoring metrics from the metrics server:

```
$ kubectl top pod web-server
NAME          CPU(cores)   MEMORY(bytes)
web-server    0m           2Mi
```

8. You can use the run command and provide the command to run as an argument. The status of the Pod will turn out to be Error:

```
$ kubectl run custom-cmd --image=busybox --restart=Never \
  -- /bin/sh -c "top-analyzer --all"
pod/custom-cmd created
$ kubectl get pod custom-cmd
NAME          READY    STATUS   RESTARTS   AGE
custom-cmd    0/1      Error    0          71s
```

9. Use the logs command to find more useful runtime information. From the error message, you'll know that the tool top-analyzer isn't available for the image:

```
$ kubectl logs custom-cmd
/bin/sh: top-analyzer: not found
```

Chapter 6, Pod Design

1. Start by creating the Pods. You can assign labels at the time of creation:

```
$ kubectl run pod-1 --image=nginx --restart=Never \
  --labels=tier=frontend,team=artemidis
pod/pod-1 created
$ kubectl run pod-2 --image=nginx --restart=Never \
  --labels=tier=backend,team=artemidis
pod/pod-2 created
$ kubectl run pod-3 --image=nginx --restart=Never \
  --labels=tier=backend,team=artemidis
pod/pod-3 created
$ kubectl get pods --show-labels
NAME    READY   STATUS    RESTARTS   AGE    LABELS
pod-1   1/1     Running   0          30s    team=artemidis,tier=frontend
pod-2   1/1     Running   0          24s    team=artemidis,tier=backend
pod-3   1/1     Running   0          16s    team=artemidis,tier=backend
```

2. You can either edit the live objects to add an annotation or use the `annotate` command. We'll use the imperative command here:

```
$ kubectl annotate pod pod-1 pod-3 deployer='Benjamin Muschko'
pod/pod-1 annotated
pod/pod-3 annotated
$ kubectl describe pod pod-1 pod-3 | grep Annotations:
Annotations:  deployer: Benjamin Muschko
Annotations:  deployer: Benjamin Muschko
```

3. The label selection requires you to combine equality- and set-based criteria to find the Pods:

```
$ kubectl get pods -l tier=backend,'team in (artemidis,aircontrol)' \
  --show-labels
NAME    READY   STATUS    RESTARTS   AGE      LABELS
pod-2   1/1     Running   0          6m38s    team=artemidis,tier=backend
pod-3   1/1     Running   0          6m30s    team=artemidis,tier=backend
```

4. The `create deployment` command creates a Deployment but doesn't allow for providing the number of replicas as a command-line option. You will have to run the `scale` command afterward:

```
$ kubectl create deployment server-deployment --image=grand-server:1.4.6
deployment.apps/server-deployment created
$ kubectl scale deployment server-deployment --replicas=2
deployment.apps/server-deployment scaled
```

5. You will find that the Deployment doesn't make any of its Pods available even after waiting for a while. The problem is that the assigned image does not exist. Having a look at one of its Pods will reveal the issue in the events log:

```
$ kubectl get deployments
NAME                     READY   UP-TO-DATE   AVAILABLE   AGE
server-deployment        0/2     2            0           69s
$ kubectl get pods
NAME                                        READY   STATUS             RESTARTS \
  AGE
server-deployment-779f77f555-q6tq2          0/1     ImagePullBackOff   0 \
  4m31s
server-deployment-779f77f555-sxtnc          0/1     ImagePullBackOff   0 \
  3m45s
$ kubectl describe pod server-deployment-779f77f555-q6tq2
...
Events:
  Type     Reason     Age                         From \
    Message
  ----     ------     ----                        ---- \
  -------
  Normal   Scheduled  <unknown>                   default-scheduler \
    Successfully assigned default/server-deployment-779f77f555-q6tq2 \
    to minikube
  Normal   Pulling    3m17s (x4 over 4m54s)  kubelet, minikube \
    Pulling image "grand-server:1.4.6"
  Warning  Failed     3m16s (x4 over 4m53s)  kubelet, minikube \
    Failed to pull image "grand-server:1.4.6": rpc error: code = \
    Unknown desc = Error response from daemon: pull access denied \
    for grand-server, repository does not exist or may require \
    'docker login': denied: requested access to the resource is denied
  Warning  Failed     3m16s (x4 over 4m53s)  kubelet, minikube \
    Error: ErrImagePull
  Normal   BackOff    3m5s (x6 over 4m53s)   kubelet, minikube \
    Back-off pulling image "grand-server:1.4.6"
  Warning  Failed     2m50s (x7 over 4m53s)  kubelet, minikube \
    Error: ImagePullBackOff
```

6. The `set image` command is a handy shortcut for assigning a new image to a Deployment. After the change, the rollout history should contain two revisions: one revision for the initial creation of the Deployment and another one for the change to the image:

```
$ kubectl set image deployment server-deployment grand-server=nginx
deployment.apps/server-deployment image updated
$ kubectl rollout history deployments server-deployment
deployment.apps/server-deployment
REVISION   CHANGE-CAUSE
1          <none>
2          <none>
```

7. You can use the image `nginx`, which has the command-line tool `curl` installed. The Unix cron expression for this job is `*/2 * * * *`:

```
$ kubectl create cronjob google-ping --schedule="*/2 * * * *" \
  --image=nginx -- /bin/sh -c 'curl google.com'
cronjob.batch/google-ping created
```

8. You can inspect when a CronJob is executed using the `-w` command-line option:

```
$ kubectl get cronjob -w
NAME          SCHEDULE       SUSPEND   ACTIVE   LAST SCHEDULE   AGE
google-ping   */2 * * * *    False     0        115s            2m10s
google-ping   */2 * * * *    False     1        6s              2m21s
google-ping   */2 * * * *    False     0        16s             2m31s
google-ping   */2 * * * *    False     1        6s              4m21s
google-ping   */2 * * * *    False     0        16s             4m31s
```

9. Explicitly assign the value 7 to the `spec.successfulJobsHistoryLimit` attribute of the live object. The resulting YAML manifest should have the following configuration:

```
...
spec:
  successfulJobsHistoryLimit: 7
...
```

10. Edit the default value of `spec.concurrencyPolicy` of the live object. The resulting YAML manifest should have the following configuration:

```
...
spec:
  concurrencyPolicy: Forbid
...
```

Chapter 7, Services and Networking

1. The fastest way to create the Pod is by using the `run` command. You can see in the following command that you can assign the port and labels at the time of creating the Pod:

```
$ kubectl run frontend --image=nginx --restart=Never --port=80 \
  -l tier=frontend,app=nginx
pod/frontend created
$ kubectl get pods
NAME       READY   STATUS    RESTARTS   AGE
frontend   1/1     Running   0          21s
```

2. Use the same method to create the backend Pod:

```
$ kubectl run backend --image=nginx --restart=Never --port=80 \
  -l tier=backend,app=nginx
pod/backend created
```

```
$ kubectl get pods
NAME        READY   STATUS    RESTARTS   AGE
backend     1/1     Running   0          19s
frontend    1/1     Running   0          3m53s
```

3. You can use the `create service` command to generate the Service. Unfortunately, you cannot assign the labels right away. Therefore, you'll write the output of the command to a YAML file and edit the label selector definition afterward:

```
$ kubectl create service clusterip nginx-service --tcp=9000:8081 \
  --dry-run=client -o yaml > nginx-service.yaml
```

Edit the YAML manifest to modify the label selector. The result should look similar to the following YAML manifest:

```
apiVersion: v1
kind: Service
metadata:
  creationTimestamp: null
  labels:
    app: nginx-service
  name: nginx-service
spec:
  ports:
  - port: 9000
    protocol: TCP
    targetPort: 8081
  selector:
    tier: backend
    deployment: app
  type: ClusterIP
status:
  loadBalancer: {}
```

Now, create the Service from the YAML file. Listing the Service should show the correct type and the exposed port:

```
$ kubectl create -f nginx-service.yaml
service/nginx-service created
$ kubectl get services
NAME            TYPE        CLUSTER-IP       EXTERNAL-IP   PORT(S)    AGE
nginx-service   ClusterIP   10.110.127.205   <none>        9000/TCP   20s
```

4. Trying to connect to the underlying Pods of the Service won't work. For example, a `wget` command times out. This behavior happens because the configuration of the Service doesn't select any Pods for two reasons. First, the label selector doesn't match any of the existing Pods. Second, the target port isn't available on any of the existing Pods:

```
$ kubectl run busybox --image=busybox --restart=Never -it --rm -- /bin/sh
/ # wget --spider --timeout=1 10.110.127.205:9000
Connecting to 10.110.127.205:9000 (10.110.127.205:9000)
```

```
wget: download timed out
/ # exit
pod "busybox" deleted
```

5. Edit the live object of the Service to look as follows. You can see in the following code snippet that the label selector was changed, as well as the target port:

```
apiVersion: v1
kind: Service
metadata:
  creationTimestamp: null
  labels:
    app: nginx-service
  name: nginx-service
spec:
  ports:
  - port: 9000
    protocol: TCP
    targetPort: 80
  selector:
    tier: backend
    app: nginx
  type: ClusterIP
status:
  loadBalancer: {}
```

As a result of the change, you will be able to connect to the backend Pod:

```
$ kubectl run busybox --image=busybox --restart=Never -it --rm -- /bin/sh
/ # wget --spider --timeout=1 10.110.127.205:9000
Connecting to 10.110.127.205:9000 (10.110.127.205:9000)
remote file exists
/ # exit
pod "busybox" deleted
```

6. You can directly modify the nginx-service live object by feeding in the desired YAML changes. Here, you're switching from the ClusterIP to the NodePort type. You can now connect to it from outside of the cluster using the node's IP address and the assigned static port:

```
$ kubectl patch service nginx-service -p \
  '{ "spec": {"type": "NodePort"} }'
service/nginx-service patched
$ kubectl get services
NAME            TYPE       CLUSTER-IP       EXTERNAL-IP   PORT(S) \
  AGE
nginx-service   NodePort   10.110.127.205   <none>        9000:32682/TCP \
  141m
$ kubectl get nodes
NAME       STATUS   ROLES    AGE     VERSION
minikube   Ready    master   102d    v1.18.3
$ kubectl describe node minikube | grep InternalIP:
```

```
  InternalIP:   192.168.64.2
$ wget --spider --timeout=1 192.168.64.2:32682
Spider mode enabled. Check if remote file exists.
--2020-09-26 15:59:12--  http://192.168.64.2:32682/
Connecting to 192.168.64.2:32682... connected.
HTTP request sent, awaiting response... 200 OK
Length: 612 [text/html]
```

7. Start by creating the namespace named `app-stack`. Copy the contents of the provided YAML definition to the file *app-stack.yaml* and apply it. You should end up with three Pods:

```
$ kubectl create namespace app-stack
namespace/app-stack created
$ kubectl apply -f app-stack.yaml
pod/frontend created
pod/backend created
pod/database created
$ kubectl get pods -n app-stack
NAME       READY   STATUS    RESTARTS   AGE
backend    1/1     Running   0          105s
database   1/1     Running   0          105s
frontend   1/1     Running   0          105s
```

8. Create a new file with the name *app-stack-network-policy.yaml*. The following rules describe the desired incoming and outgoing traffic for the `database` Pod:

```
apiVersion: networking.k8s.io/v1
kind: NetworkPolicy
metadata:
  name: app-stack-network-policy
  namespace: app-stack
spec:
  podSelector:
    matchLabels:
      app: todo
      tier: database
  policyTypes:
  - Ingress
  - Egress
  ingress:
  - from:
    - podSelector:
        matchLabels:
          app: todo
          tier: backend
```

Apply the YAML file using the following command:

```
$ kubectl create -f app-stack-network-policy.yaml
networkpolicy.networking.k8s.io/app-stack-network-policy created
$ kubectl get networkpolicy -n app-stack
```

```
NAME                          POD-SELECTOR              AGE
app-stack-network-policy      app=todo,tier=database    7s
```

9. You can further restrict the ports with the following definition:

```
apiVersion: networking.k8s.io/v1
kind: NetworkPolicy
metadata:
  name: app-stack-network-policy
  namespace: app-stack
spec:
  podSelector:
    matchLabels:
      app: todo
      tier: database
  policyTypes:
  - Ingress
  - Egress
  ingress:
  - from:
    - podSelector:
        matchLabels:
          app: todo
          tier: backend
    ports:
    - protocol: TCP
      port: 3306
```

The `describe` command can verify that the correct port ingress rule has been applied:

```
$ kubectl describe networkpolicy app-stack-network-policy -n app-stack
Name:         app-stack-network-policy
Namespace:    app-stack
Created on:   2020-09-27 16:22:31 -0600 MDT
Labels:       <none>
Annotations:  <none>
Spec:
  PodSelector:     app=todo,tier=database
  Allowing ingress traffic:
    To Port: 3306/TCP
    From:
      PodSelector: app=todo,tier=backend
  Allowing egress traffic:
    <none> (Selected pods are isolated for egress connectivity)
  Policy Types: Ingress, Egress
```

Chapter 8, State Persistence

1. Start by generating the YAML manifest using the `run` command in combination with the `--dry-run` option:

   ```
   $ kubectl run alpine --image=alpine:3.12.0 --dry-run=client \
     --restart=Never -o yaml -- /bin/sh -c "while true; do sleep 60; \
     done;" > multi-container-alpine.yaml
   $ vim multi-container-alpine.yaml
   ```

   After editing the Pod, the manifest could look as follows. The container names here are `container1` and `container2`:

   ```yaml
   apiVersion: v1
   kind: Pod
   metadata:
     creationTimestamp: null
     labels:
       run: alpine
     name: alpine
   spec:
     containers:
     - args:
       - /bin/sh
       - -c
       - while true; do sleep 60; done;
       image: alpine:3.12.0
       name: container1
       resources: {}
     - args:
       - /bin/sh
       - -c
       - while true; do sleep 60; done;
       image: alpine:3.12.0
       name: container2
       resources: {}
     dnsPolicy: ClusterFirst
     restartPolicy: Always
   status: {}
   ```

2. Edit the YAML file further by adding the Volume and the mount paths for both containers.

   In the end, the Pod definition could look as follows:

   ```yaml
   apiVersion: v1
   kind: Pod
   metadata:
     creationTimestamp: null
     labels:
       run: alpine
   ```

```
    name: alpine
spec:
  volumes:
  - name: shared-vol
    emptyDir: {}
  containers:
  - args:
    - /bin/sh
    - -c
    - while true; do sleep 60; done;
    image: alpine:3.12.0
    name: container1
    volumeMounts:
    - name: shared-vol
      mountPath: /etc/a
    resources: {}
  - args:
    - /bin/sh
    - -c
    - while true; do sleep 60; done;
    image: alpine:3.12.0
    name: container2
    volumeMounts:
    - name: shared-vol
      mountPath: /etc/b
    resources: {}
  dnsPolicy: ClusterFirst
  restartPolicy: Always
status: {}
```

Create the Pod and check if it has been created properly. You should see the Pod in Running status with two containers ready:

```
$ kubectl create -f multi-container-alpine.yaml
pod/alpine created
$ kubectl get pods
NAME      READY   STATUS    RESTARTS   AGE
alpine    2/2     Running   0          18s
```

3. Use the exec command to shell into the container named container1. Create the file */etc/a/data/hello.txt* with the relevant content:

```
$ kubectl exec alpine -c container1 -it -- /bin/sh
/ # cd /etc/a
/etc/a # ls -l
total 0
/etc/a # mkdir data
/etc/a # cd data/
/etc/a/data # echo "Hello World" > hello.txt
/etc/a/data # cat hello.txt
```

```
Hello World
/etc/a/data # exit
```

4. Use the `exec` command to shell into the container named `container2`. The contents of the file */etc/b/data/hello.txt* should say "Hello World":

```
$ kubectl exec alpine -c container2 -it -- /bin/sh
/ # cat /etc/b/data/hello.txt
Hello World
/ # exit
```

5. Start by creating a new file named *logs-pv.yaml*. The contents could look as follows:

```
kind: PersistentVolume
apiVersion: v1
metadata:
  name: logs-pv
spec:
  capacity:
    storage: 5Gi
  accessModes:
    - ReadWriteOnce
    - ReadOnlyMany
  hostPath:
    path: /var/logs
```

Create the PersistentVolume object and check on its status:

```
$ kubectl create -f logs-pv.yaml
persistentvolume/logs-pv created
$ kubectl get pv
NAME       CAPACITY   ACCESS MODES   RECLAIM POLICY   STATUS      CLAIM \
    STORAGECLASS   REASON   AGE
logs-pv    5Gi        RWO,ROX        Retain           Available \
                        18s
```

6. Create the file *logs-pvc.yaml* to define the PersistentVolumeClaim. The following YAML manifest shows its contents:

```
kind: PersistentVolumeClaim
apiVersion: v1
metadata:
  name: logs-pvc
spec:
  accessModes:
    - ReadWriteOnce
  resources:
    requests:
      storage: 2Gi
```

Create the PersistentVolume object and check on its status:

```
$ kubectl create -f logs-pvc.yaml
persistentvolumeclaim/logs-pvc created
$ kubectl get pvc
NAME       STATUS   VOLUME                                    CAPACITY \
  ACCESS MODES   STORAGECLASS   AGE
logs-pvc   Bound    pvc-47ac2593-2cd2-4213-9e31-450bc98bb43f   2Gi \
  RWO              standard       11s
```

7. Create the basic YAML manifest using the `--dry-run` command-line option:

```
$ kubectl run nginx --image=nginx --dry-run=client --restart=Never \
  -o yaml > nginx-pod.yaml
```

Now, edit the file *nginx-pod.yaml* and bind the PersistentVolumeClaim to it:

```
apiVersion: v1
kind: Pod
metadata:
  creationTimestamp: null
  labels:
    run: nginx
  name: nginx
spec:
  volumes:
    - name: logs-volume
      persistentVolumeClaim:
        claimName: logs-pvc
  containers:
  - image: nginx
    name: nginx
    volumeMounts:
      - mountPath: "/var/log/nginx"
        name: logs-volume
    resources: {}
  dnsPolicy: ClusterFirst
  restartPolicy: Never
status: {}
```

Create the Pod using the following command and check its status:

```
$ kubectl create -f nginx-pod.yaml
pod/nginx created
$ kubectl get pods
NAME    READY   STATUS    RESTARTS   AGE
nginx   1/1     Running   0          8s
```

8. Use the `exec` command to open an interactive shell to the Pod and create a file in the mounted directory:

```
$ kubectl exec nginx -it -- /bin/sh
# cd /var/log/nginx
# touch my-nginx.log
# ls
```

```
access.log  error.log  my-nginx.log
# exit
```

9. After re-creating the Pod, the file stored on the PersistentVolume should still exist:

```
$ kubectl delete pod nginx
$ kubectl create -f nginx-pod.yaml
pod/nginx created
$ kubectl exec nginx -it -- /bin/sh
# cd /var/log/nginx
# ls
access.log  error.log  my-nginx.log
# exit
```

Index

About the Author

Benjamin Muschko is a software engineer, consultant, and trainer with more than 15 years of experience in the industry. He's passionate about project automation, testing, and continuous delivery. Ben is an author, a frequent speaker at conferences, and an avid open source advocate. He holds the CKAD certification.

Software projects sometimes feel like climbing a mountain. In his free time, Ben loves hiking Colorado's 14ers (*https://www.14ers.com*) and enjoys conquering long-distance trails.

Colophon

The animal on the cover of *Certified Kubernetes Application Developer (CKAD) Study Guide* is a common porpoise (*Phocoena phocoena*). It is the smallest of the seven [.keep-together]#species# of porpoise and one of the smallest marine mammals. Adults are 4.5 to 6 feet long and weigh between 130 and 170 pounds. They are dark gray with lightly speckled sides and white undersides. Females are larger than males.

The common porpoise lives in the coastal waters of the North Atlantic, North Pacific, and Black Sea. They are also known as harbor porpoises since they inhabit fjords, bays, estuaries, and harbors. These marine mammals eat very small schooling fish and will hunt several hundred fish per hour throughout the day. They are usually solitary hunters but will occasionally form small packs.

Porpoises use ultrasonic clicks for echolocation (for both navigation and hunting) and social communication. A mass of adipose tissue in the skull, known as a melon, focuses and modulates their vocalizations.

Porpoises are conscious breathers, so if they are unconscious for a long time, they may drown. In captivity, they have been known to sleep with one side of their brain at a time so that they can still swim and breathe consciously.

The conservation status of the common porpoise is of least concern. Many of the animals on O'Reilly covers are endangered; all of them are important to the world.

The cover illustration is by Karen Montgomery, based on a black and white engraving from *British Quadrupeds*. The cover fonts are Gilroy Semibold and Guardian Sans. The text font is Adobe Minion Pro; the heading font is Adobe Myriad Condensed; and the code font is Dalton Maag's Ubuntu Mono.

O'REILLY®

There's much more where this came from.

Experience books, videos, live online training courses, and more from O'Reilly and our 200+ partners—all in one place.

Learn more at oreilly.com/online-learning

CPSIA information can be obtained
at www.ICGtesting.com
Printed in the USA
JSHW052045140721
16908JS00005B/242